Edited by Gill Calvert, Jill Morgan and Mouse Katz

Pandora's Box

Special thanks

To early members of the Womens Images committee for the work they contributed: Helen Cherry, Helen White, Elana Samperi, LillAnn Chepstows Lusty.

For giving generously of their time, and experience in support, advice and assistance: Hilary Lane, Mike Sixsmith, Leslie Green, Beverly Huey, Jacqueline Morreau, Phillippa Brooster & staff, Liz Lydiate, Suzanne Perkins, Mary Parker, Sarah Lefanu, Melanie Hart, Sarah Wilson, Denise Hooker, Nicky Bird, Graham Bush, Tassie Russell, Jacky Ford, Pauline Barrie, Zoe DeRopp, Joyce Agee, Lewis Biggs, Clive Barger, Catherine Carey-Elwis, Dieter Bauer, Lynda Harris.

To Conway Lloyd Morgan.

To Jill Morgan, Bev Bytheway and staff of Rochdale Art Gallery.

To all the artists, too numerous to include, who sent their work and encouragement.

And to the 32 participating artists, without whom this exhibition would not have been possible.

This exhibition was generously supported by the Arts Council of Great Britain and the Greater London Arts Association.

Produced and distributed by Trefoil Books Ltd, of Royal Parade, Dawes Road, London SW7, for the Rochdale Art Gallery and Womens Images.

Editorial assistance: Denise Hooker

Photography: Graham Bush (except for work by Peggie Radford, Sarah Pirozek, Penny Woolcock, Helen Ganly, Linda Black, Joyce Agee, Joan Wakelin, Christine Voge, Lois Williams, Alison Allnutt)

Printed and bound by Van Leer

First published 1984

Published on the occasion of the exhibition *Pandora's Box*.

Contents

Introductions

Works & Statements

(Colour illustrations appear on pages 9-12, 29-32, 49-52, 61-62, 71-74, 83-84, and 93-96)

DENISE HOOKER
A Fresh Look

The artists brought together in this exhibition come from a wide variety of backgrounds and countries, each necessarily bringing their different individual experiences to bear on their personal interpretations of the myth of Pandora's Box. Just as the highly successful precursor to this show, *Women's Images of Men*, turned the tables on the male artistic tradition and made men the object of the female gaze, so this exhibition aims to give women's view of a theme which has provided inspiration for male artists throughout the centuries. A contemporary work by the German artist Hans Haacke confirms the continuing vitality of the myth and its lasting power over the creative imagination. In his overtly critical portrait of Mrs. Thatcher, seen earlier this year at the Tate Gallery, the Prime Minister is depicted seated next to a table on which stands a late Victorian statue of Pandora about to open her box and release all the miseries into the world. The artist's meaning is clear. He is the most recent of a long line of men who have taken the myth on face value to represent woman as the source of all evil. As such, it has had a powerful influence in culturally determining the historically negative view of the female.

The artists in this show take a fresh look at the myth and demonstrate that it is capable of sustaining radically different interpretations unprejudicial to women. They variously challenge the received view of Pandora and enlarge upon her significance as an image for women today. Although differing widely in style and using a variety of media, all the works are to a greater or lesser extent figurative. This stems from a conscious desire on the part of the artists to reach a larger audience than the traditional gallery-going public. They feel that they have something urgent to say and wish to place their work within a broader social context.

The parallels between the stories of Pandora and Eve are evident. By opening the box, or eating the apple, they introduced evil into the world and innocence was lost forever. The two figures are interchangeable in many of the works in the exhibition. The fatal consequences for mankind of Pandora/Eve's action are shown in a photograph by Kathleen Michael which incorporates a sculpture of Adam and Eve being driven out of Paradise. Jacqueline Morreau depicts an anguished Adam and Eve inseparably entwined within the apple, falling through a dark abyss. Pandora, like Eve, is seen to be used as a scapegoat by men to absolve them of any responsibility or blame for the world's evils. Representations of Pandora/Eve by Alison Allnutt, Sonia York and Mary McGowan underline her essential innocence by their use of the brightly coloured, simplified style of children's comics, book illustrations and drawings.

Many of the artists choose to concentrate on the evils that were released from the box, their work constituting a biting indictment of male misuse of political, economic and religious power. Hilary Rosen graphically depicts the miseries of modern urban life in images of poverty, torture, alcoholism, domestic violence and world conflict. Tessa Pollit places her personifications of the 'seven deadly sins' within a political framework. Death, destruction and the threat of nuclear warfare predominate. Soldiers are manipulated like puppets in the work of June Raby and Bernadette O'Donohue to symbolise the military manoeuverings and jostling for position by the world powers. The individual is merely an insignificant pawn in such political games. Not all the artists treat the theme literally. Jane Lewis' slaughterhouse vision of exploitation is macabrely surrealist, while Peggie Radford's good humoured parody of male erotic fantasy has a darker side. The initial amusement provoked by her nearly life-sized, scantily clad ice cream vendor quickly turns sour when the viewer realises that the phallic ice cream cones which she so audaciously proffers are topped with the gas-masked heads of soldiers. Katya Coupland's brightly coloured image of an exploding handbag is a witty contemporary metaphor for the opening of Pandora's box, with all the attractive slickness and bland deception of an advertisement.

Pandora/Eve's action marks the moment of transition from the natural, instinctual life to an awareness of good and evil. Seen in this light, the opening of the box becomes for many of the artists a positive action, an assertion of human freedom. Pandora is transformed into a prototype existential heroine who deliberately and consciously chooses to open the box in a quest for knowledge and understanding of the full range of human experience. Joanne Woodward's *Erasmian Pyxis* depicts the story of the myth and its present-day consequences on the panels of a box which opens to reveal a jar – the original box – symbol of the hope that remained. Bernadette O'Donohue shows Pandora gazing into a crystal ball. She represents the feminine principle associated with those life-affirming qualities which are the only hope for the future of mankind. Joan Wakelin and Hilary Rosen find tangible expression of this hope in the Peace Movement and the Greenham Common women. Catherine McWilliams' brightly coloured figure of Pandora in *Woman with Peace Line* relates directly to her hope for the end of sectarian violence in Northern Ireland.

Other artists have chosen to examine the effects that the negative attitudes towards women expressed in the myth have had on their lives. Their inferior status is depicted in Gillian Calvert's *Women's Estate*, which protrays women's traditional roles of cleaning and caring for children, providing those essential but undervalued services which maintain the fabric of society. Dierdre Shulman's *Jessica* considers how social conditioning shapes and limits women's aspirations. Even so-called liberated women find themselves trapped in traditional roles. The commentary accompanying Sarah Pirozek's series of photographs based on clothes-washing wrily and wittily juxtaposes the rhetoric of consicousness-raising

Pascale Petite
Ancestral Memory
Mixed media

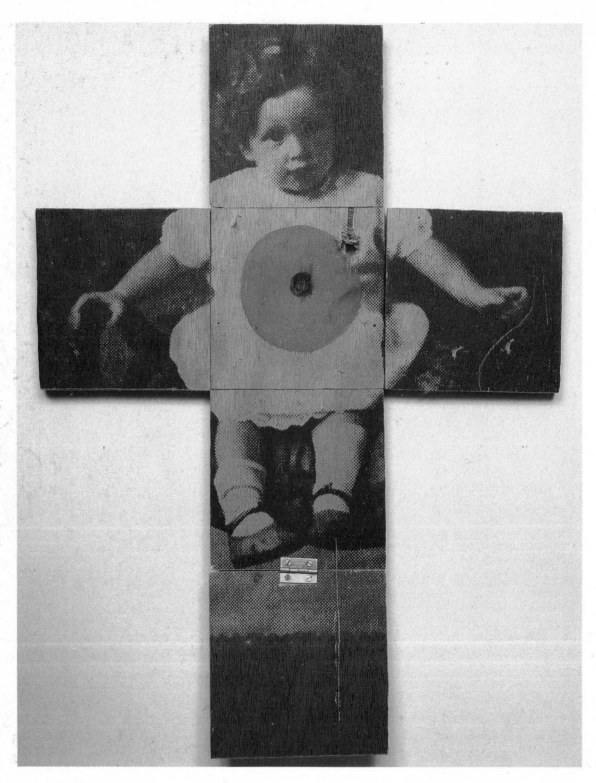

Bernadette O'Donohue
Pandora's Box: A Child of Yesterday
Screen-print on plywood

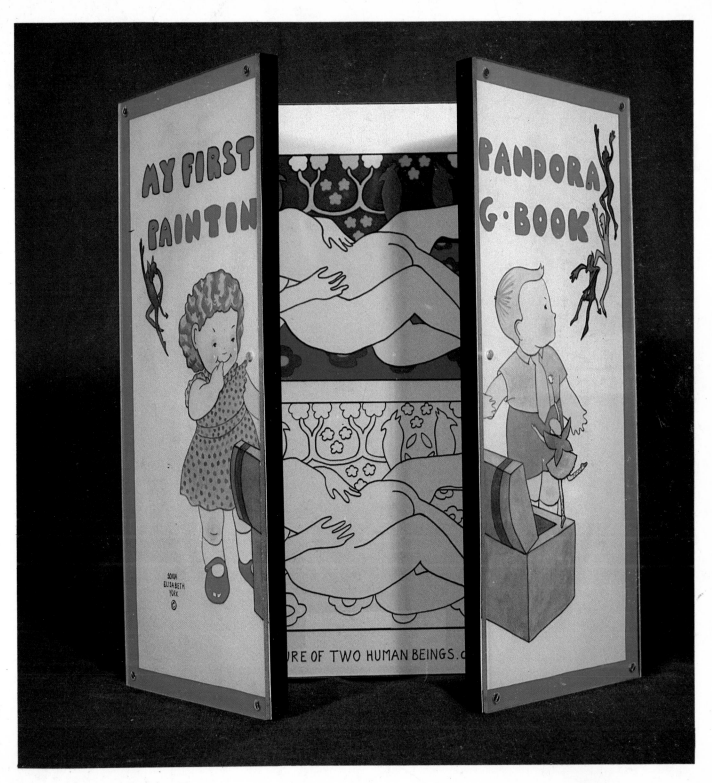

Sonia York
My First Pandora Painting Book
Watercolour, 14 x 12 ins.

with domestic reality. The women in Elana Samperi's work are angrily trying to break out of the prison-boxes of their homes, while in Maria Chevska's intensely anguished paintings lost and isolated figures seek to escape the boundaries of the strange nightmarish limbo which surrounds and confines them.

Pandora's box is seen by many as the source of all life, a natural symbol for the womb. Jacqueline Morreau's *She Who Spins* embodies the power of the feminine in the form of one of the three classical Fates who wove the web of man's life and destiny from her own body. The myth of Pandora can clearly be read as an expression of male fear and distrust of female sexuality. Jane Lewis' grotesque child-woman dancing with the decapitated head of a man in a parody of seductiveness makes an explicit comparison between Pandora and the equally fatal Salome. Deborah Monroe's series of photo-etchings can be variously interpreted depending on the order in which they are presented. As shown in the catalogue, the incorporation of the box into the woman's body is a positive expression of the all-embracing power of female sexuality and fertility. Seen in reverse order, the works become a visual metaphor for men's efforts to control and contain the feared feminine. The woman squatting in a position of fertility is gradully completely obliterated by the enveloping box. Onto that blank screen men project their own sexual fantasies which effectively preclude the possibility of any real communication. Penny Woolcock's incorporation of pornographic imagery into her work shows women acquiescing in this process by their conformity to male stereotypes.

The gulf between the sexes and the complex power struggles involved are poignantly captured in Christine Voge's photograph of a black man reaching out to touch the leg of a white stripper. Joyce Agee's photographs of women watching a male stripper provide an interesting contrast with men's attitudes. Any element of eroticism is diffused by the women's laughter at the reversal of the usual roles and the comic reflection of their own sexual behaviour seen in the distorting mirror of the male stripper. Women's lack of any clear sense of their own identity independent of men is the subject of a deceptively whimsical work by Linda Black. In *Dressing Table* she shows a woman adorned with feminine frills and flowers gazing into a mirror. But no image is reflected back, only three birds fluttering away in a romantic dream as insubstantial as herself. This sense of female invisibility is also apparent in Pascale Petit's full size figure of Pandora staring into a mirror. She is translucent, a glass woman. It is her unconscious self which is reflected back.

The influence of Jungian psychology is discernible in those artists who interpret the opening of Pandora's box as an attempt to get in touch with the contents of the unconscious and discover the full female potential. Pascale Petit's glass sculpture *Ancestral Memory*

Lois Williams
The Black Garden
Mixed media

is a haunting image of the unconscious as a multilayered storehouse of experience. Janine Lajudie similarly presents the unknown dimension of the unconscious as a transparent, lockable glass box. Mouse Katz' work has a richly symbolic content and uses a wide range of imagery from ancient Greek, Egyptian and Medieval Christian art to embody the feminine principle. Her series of four boxes have a striking theatricality. The lid of the Egyptian box opens to reveal Pandora as the dazzling Phoenix, the bird of hope, rising out of the depths of the unconscious, joining inner and outer. Helen Ganly's ornate, double-sided hanging figure of Pandora represents the *anima*, the feminine part of the personality which connects with the unconscious.

Some of the artists have challenged the negative implications of the Pandora story by unearthing parallel creation myths which show women as a positive force for good, the giver of all life. Marisa Rueda's work, which is directly related to the political situation in South America, is based on the Argentinian myth of Akewa, the sun goddess. She is the sole survivor of the original race of women who dwelt in heaven when men were still four-legged fur-covered beasts; a symbol of freedom from male oppression and abuse of power. Elana Samperi refers to the Panamanian myth of the Goddess Mu, the giant blue butterfly lady who gave birth to the universe and created everything that exists. In *Inside the Box* woman – once the Goddess Mu – is pinioned to the wall, screaming in horror and protest at being trapped within the box, ensnared and subordinated by men. Louise Baker goes back to an earlier version of the Pandora myth which sees her as the original Earth Mother. Her box opens to reveal many drawers divided into compartments like an archeological display case whose contents show women as fertility goddesses, the original creators and harvesters, the source of all knowledge.

Not all the artists have chosen to deal directly with the story of Pandora. Lois Williams avoids the explicitly narrative and uses the myth as visual stimulus for her investigations of the more formal sculptural possibilities suggested by the theme.

Underlying the wide variety of interpretations of the myth there are certain recurrent images such as a woman's open-mouthed scream of protest; mutilated, bleeding bodies; mirrors and puppets. They indicate fundamental preoccupations common to many of the artists, particularly their resentment of male misuse of power and the denial of the full development of female potential. Seen collectively, the works in this exhibition represent an attempt to establish a sense of women's identity and the positive role they can play in shaping the future.

LYNDA HARRIS

The Myth of Pandora and Women's changing Image

The theme of this exhibition is well chosen, for the myth of Pandora and its variations are a key to women's images over the years.

If we look first at the earliest known traces of Pandora, we discover that she was originally a form of Ge, or Gaia, the Earth Goddess. Her name, Pandora or Anesidora, meant the all-giving, or the sender-forth of gifts.[5] She was the Earth Mother: the giver of abundance and life, vegetable, animal and human.

Persephone and Pandora symbolisedl the death and rebirth of vegetation, and also the death and rebirth of human beings. They were identified with the earth which was thought of as the Mother, from which all life comes, and to which it all cyclically returns. Closely associated with these concepts was the *pithos*, a large urn or storage jar. This *pithos* was Pandora's original container in the well known myth. It did not acquire a square boxlike shape until the Renaissance.[6] The *pithos* may even have been identified with Pandora from the very early period when she was an Earth Goddess. Its shape was not unlike that of a woman. It was used to store grain and other edibles identified in the ancient world with rebirth. It was also sometimes used for burials of the dead[2]. Like Pandora, it was thus associated with birth and death. Both Pandora and the *pithos* seem to have been thought of as the body or womb of the earth, in which all mortal beings were buried, and from which (like the grain) they would someday be born into another life.

The *pithos*, or urn is very much a female symbol. It is the womb, the female genitals, the mouth, the entire female body. Its associations with the mouth connect it with many female figures in mythology who were also swallowers. In Egypt, the symbolism was gentle and positive – the sky goddess Nut ate the sun at sunset, and the soul at death. Both were later reborn gloriously from her 'belly'. But in other cultures, such as Babylon or Greece, similar female images were often terrifying. The Greek sphinx, for example, lived in a cave. She seduced men into it with her riddles, and then ate them, leaving the bones. The Sirens enticed men with their songs for the purpose of devouring them. The sepentine female Lamia was another voracious monster. Such creatures were prototypes for vampires, or even the Medieval mouth of Hell, swallower of souls.[9]

The ancient images of female as voracious reflect men's feelings that women are irresistible yet dangerous. These fears and feelings still exist today, and various psychological reasons have been suggested to explain them, including a fear of castration due to female penis envy, an association of sex with death (the male organ 'dies' as its sperm is lost), and childhood associations of the mother with both love and anger.[10]

All these suggestions may make sense. But even more potent, perhaps, are our half-buried memories of the Mother Goddess. The

Goddess (of whom, as we've seen, Pandora was once one form) had two aspects. On the one hand she was associated with the bright, upper world of vegetation and growth. This side of her personified beauty, sexual attractiveness, love, tenderness, wisdom, the growth of crops and birth of babies. In her other aspect she was the dark mother – mistress of the cavelike underworld, of death, of spirits and the violent swallowing of life. Along with these beliefs went rituals that seem utterly horrifying to us today. Men could b literally torn apart and even eaten by frenzied women. Various myths that have come down to us reflect these rites. Among them are the stories concerning Adonis, Actaeon, Dionysos and Pentheus.[2] It is not surprising that men feared women in the past, and that some of these fears still linger on today. √

The ancient religion of the Mother Goddess goes back tens of thousands of years. It appears to have existed all over the world, as far back as human remains can be traced. This means that for most of human history a female was the chief deity – the equivalent of today's God the Father. This situation began to alter in about 3,000 B.C., only comparatively recently from a historical point of view. But it has altered so completely that we only very vaguely remember the old religion. The changes began when tribes from Northeast Europe (perhaps originally from the Caucasus) invaded Europe and India. They brought with them the skill of writing, a prejudice against dark skins and a dominant male sky god. Probably they also brought a social change, for there is evidence that in the early periods, women rather than men were the ruling figures in society.[8] Their ancient domination, based on mythology, magic and intuition, was gradually overcome by the males' physical strength and rational, 'left brain' approach.

The later myth of Pandora and her urn or box, which is so well known today, is a direct product of the new male-dominated religion and the new male-dominated society. It was invented (or first written down) by the Greek poet Hesiod, in about 700 B.C. Hesiod lived in a time when the Goddess religion had waned, but was not yet entirely gone. He helped to weaken it further by changing the powerful, ancient Earth Goddess Pandora into a mischievous and pernicious human female. One can see the story as an attempt to transform woman's menacing side into something admittedly evil, but at the same time weak and inferior. A kind of male self-protection, which is perhaps understandable, in view of the fearful side of the Goddess, and some of the very bloodthirsty women's rituals which still existed in Hesiod's day. Hesiod's tale blames Pandora for the world's evils, but at the same time tames her.

In Hesiod's story, Zeus (who by this time was the dominant male deity) was angry at men for acquiring fire. So he had Hephaistos (another male god who had taken over a previously female role) create a maiden out of earth and water. This was the first woman: Pandora. Athene, Aphrodite and other female deities gave her beauty, clothes, skills and charms. Her qualities also included lies and cunning ways, given to her by Hermes. Her name was now interpreted as meaning the all-gifted. She had become a passive receiver of gifts, and was no longer a giver of bounty.

Pandora was both beautiful and evil – a 'trap, deadly to men'.[4] Like the ancient Mother Goddess she had two sides, but unlike her, she was weak, and not worthy of men's respect. Hermes brought her to Epimetheus, the brother of Prometheus who had given fire to men. Epimetheus forgot his brother's warning that he shoudl take no gifts from Zeus, and accepted her. It was not long after this that Pandora opened the forbidden urn. It had been filled by Prometheus with all earth's evils, pains and diseases. When closed, it kept these away from men. But Pandora, seen by Hesiod as a foolish trouble-maker, let them out. Only Hope remained within. The urn itself, a symbol of the female body, makes Hesiod's meaning even more plain: women are tempting on the outside, but evil within, and all the world's troubles come from them. In this context, the 'hope' that remained within the urn perhaps symbolised the one thing about women that Hesiod really valued: their ability to have children.

Hesiod's myth was taken up by the Fathers of the Church, who compared Pandora to Eve.[6] The two women had much in common. Both were fatally beautiful, and both were weak, foolish trouble-makers. They caused death and evils to overwhelm mankind, but they also played a valuable role in that they bore children. The Goddess had now been totally transformed, from a powerful creator, into a weak vessel, who played a useful role in a world dominated by men. The ancient myths in which the Goddess had lingered on as Artemis, Persephone or Aphrodite, among others, were no longer taken seriously. Some of the Goddess's positive qualities had been transferred to the Virgin Mary, but Mary was always seen as subservient to Jesus and God the Father.

The myth of Pandora became a popular subject in art and poetry during the Renaissance. By this time the Mother Goddess was less well remembered, and men were able to relent a little in their image of Pandora. She was now sometimes shown with two containers – one of good, and one of evil. The painting *Eva Prima Pandora* by the sixteenth century French artist Jean Cousin, now in the Louvre, is one example of this approach. There were even occasions when Pandora's urn or box held only good things, as in a Parisian tableau of 1549.[6] More often, however, Hesiod's story remained basically unchanged. This situation continued through-out the Renaissance, and during the centuries that followed.

Today, when women's images and self-images are changing, the myth of Pandora begins to look different. Are women really such an extreme contrast of dark and light; positive and negative? Why should we not see ourselves simply as people? Are we really so different from men? Many people today believe that each of us, whatever our gender, contains both 'male' and 'female' qualities. Men can be gentle and nurturing; women can be aggressive and efficient.

But it would be regrettable if women now went too far and forgot what can be seen as the lessons of the myth of Pandora. As was said earlier, what lies behind this myth may not be a disrespect for women, but a great fear of them. There are certainly many hints of this fear. It may date from a period, long ago, when women, then dominant, misused their power. The fearful mythological images of the Mother's dark side, and the records of violent rites, directed towards males, seem to be evidence of a kind of rulership that needed to be overthrown.

Now, after many centuries of male suppression, women seem to have outgrown their ancient violence. Perhaps the time has come for a new version of the myth of Pandora to be written. In this one, Pandora would be more like the Egyptian mother goddesses Nut, Harthor and Isis: strong, equal with men, gentle, positive and life-enhancing. Her urn would not be a blood-thirsty devourer, and it would not release violent or evil spirits. Instead, it would be a source of nourishment and bounty – a symbol of birth and rebirth in a totally positive sense.

Bibliography and Notes

1. J.E. Cirlot, *A Dictionary of Symbols*, N.Y., 1962
2. Robert Graves, *The Greek Myths*, vols 1 and 2, Penguin, 1960
3. Jane Harrison, 'Pandora's Box', *Journal of Hellenic Studies*, XX (1900)
4. Hesiod, *Theogony* and *Works and Days*, Penguin, 1973
5. C. Kerenyi, *The Gods of the Greeks*, Thames and Hudson, 1979
6. Dora and Erwin Panofsky, *Pandora's Box*, Bollingen, 1962
7. Mary Renault, *The King Must Die*, Longmans, 1958
8. Merlin Stone, *When God was a Woman*, Harvest, 1976 (Virago title: *The Paradise Papers*)
9. Emily Vermeule, *Death in Early Greek Art and Poetry*, U. Cal., 1981
10. Rex Warner et al, *Encyclopedia of World Mythology*, Peerage, 1975

JACQUELINE MORREAU
Gaining Ground

The last 14 years have seen some hopeful changes in attitudes towards women artists. Although this does not mean that they have won their place in the public consciousness, let alone in the annals of art history, it does mean that the massive efforts they have made to gain visibility both in England and in the United States, have not been made in vain. When women got together to analyse the problem, they were able to take a fresh look at what women were doing and why, and then to take positive action to produce these changes.

Before the impact of the Women's Movement was felt by artists, there was amongst them the tendency to blame themselves for being left out of the art 'scene'. The renaissance for women began when, in *Art and Sexual Politics*, published in 1970, Linda Nochlin asked the provocative question: 'Why have there been no great women artists?'

One response was to reject the question and to excavate and therefore retrieve artists who had been lost to history, artists lost for centuries like Artemesia Gentileschi, Sofonisba Anguisola etc, for decades, like Gwen John, and some still alive, unrecognised except by the few. Georgia O'Keefe was 'rediscovered', as was Alice Neal. In England, new attention was paid to the work of Barbara Hepworth, for instance. But what about artists still working and trying to find an audience for their work? It was not seen as the role of the historian to judge the present. Among historians, though, there was the belief that 'greatness' *was* a meaningful quality, and that many women had had and do have it.

Others, however, began by questioning at a deeper level what 'great' meant; who decides what art represents whom; who preserves what work and makes it available to future generations, and why.

We have been able to see in our own lifetime how unpopular ideas are suppresed. We can see how artists' work has been used for purposes for which it was not intended[1]. From this knowledge, it was not hard to begin to understand how women had been locked out of the art 'scene' of our time, especially where female meanings were apparent in the work. But more than that, women were beginning to see how they had to conform to, and to be accepted in, the masculine art world.

Furthermore, this repression of their own meanings had turned many women artists against themselves, had turned the work sour. Work gave little pleasure, the drive needed for continuous effort was lost for lack of audience and feedback.

Other women were suffering from the more fundamental problem of how to manage when cultural pressures, as well as internal ones, prevented them from working effectively: raising children, work, lack of space, and above all the lack of any recognition of the validity of their right to pursue their own careers, prevented work from being born.

Above all, women began to realise that they could never be considered 'great' or even good 'artists' as long as 'great' and 'artist' were terms pertaining only to the male.

Lucy Lippard, in 'From the centre' gives ten reasons why women cannot 'make it' in the art world. And these are still valid today, nearly ten years after the publication of her book.

With a new clarity, a woman could now begin to understand why men did not want to be made aware of her experience of reality. It represented aspects of himself that he had repressed (Susan Griffith, 1980 'Pornography and Silence'). As women gained new awareness of the 'dominant/muted' aspect of the male/female relationships (Dale Spender, 1980, 'Man Made Language') the woman artist could begin to untangle the roots of her repression, and begin a whole new period of growth for herself and her work.

She was able to admit, now, that much of her acceptance and admiration of the work by men, had been made possible through the kind of displacement of her own identity, (from female to pseudo-male) which was essential for the appreciation of so many cultural artifacts.

Woman had also to become men in their imaginations so as to be able to be active, positive and in control and to identify with the hero or maker. Women began looking for work which interested them, and artists began to look for an audience to address who would respond to their work.

The answer to the question: 'To whom do we address our work?' was obviously 'other women'.

Thus a period of autobiographical work began. The phrase 'the personal is political' galvanised women into action. The clothes they wore, the dishes they washed, the poverty women felt, the displacement, the lack of choice, the lack of value attached to their work as women, all these became valid subjects for works of visual art, theatre, and literature.

Women reclaimed their own bodies for their own experience and use. The artists began to question the cultural assumptions which had arisen not out of women's own experience, but out of men's observation of that experience.

Menstruation, the moods and changes were seen in their positive aspects, as well as their mysterious, even threatening ones (Cate Elwes performance, 1978). Examination of social constructs of femininity, i.e. make-up, high-heeled shoes, long finger nails (Alexis Hunter, 1976, 1977). The subject of the artist as housewife made an explosive, entertaining and instructive theme show when displayed at the Institute of Contemporary Arts in 1978, as the 'Feministo' show. This exhibition consisted of work on a small scale which women had sent to each other by post. This demonstrated to the public some of the problems for women artists when confined to the home, torn between loving, caring for the family, and the need to continue their own work.

Some artists took on these questions and changed their practice to avoid these traps. They tried to work anonymously, in groups, and without individual styles. Some also returned to specifically 'female' identified media such as sewing and embroidery and charged these with feminist meanings.

But most artists continued to work in areas familiar to them, not wishing to give up useful skills and techniques to which they were visually committed. However, they tried to encompass female meaning more overtly and specifically than they could have done before the women's movement.

Where they could not so adapt them, the styles and techniques changed organically to encompass new needs. This leads to work in which visual pleasure was not denied, but was used to lead the viewer into new areas of thought, unlike the barriers which conceptual art, much used then by feminists, imposed.

Other artists wished to use new media which did not have a long history of masculine meanings: performance, video, etc. Rose Garrard's performance 'Beyond Still Life' (1980) filled the myth of Pandora with new meanings and was the forerunner of the kind of re-examination of myths and clichés about women embodied in the present exhibition.

In the 1970's the Womens Arts Alliance Gallery, under the direction of Linda Mallet and Jenni Norris was the focus for political/feminist shows. A wide range of styles were used by women around a central, but not too specific theme. This demonstrated how theme shows could create a context for female meanings. 'Off the Fence', 'Women's Images of Women' and many other shows demonstrated for the first time for many artists that work could be shown without losing a battle against cultural assumptions about art and the identity of the artist, within a 'theme' show.

This very small gallery, however, could not accommodate the increasing numbers of women artists needing to show their work. An additional problem was that the wider public were often afraid to come to an overtly feminist space. Often the work was seen only, and appreciated by, the already converted, and although this was an extremely important aspect of the work, it was still not enough to change public attitudes towards women's meanings.

Out of the exhibition came slide shows, discussions and meetings, and ideas for an intervention into the larger art world began to form.

Meanwhile a group of women more associated with the then mainstream styles of expression compaigned to select the important Hayward Annual (1978). They succeeded in this, and chose an exhibition which included the work of Mary Kelly, Susan Hiller and Alexis Hunter.

Alexis Hunter was responsible too for organising a slide show at the Hayward to which any woman artist could bring work to display and discuss. This event lasted about eight hours and was extremely useful and informative to many artists and organisers of future events, particularly to those women who were already in the process of organising 'Women's Images of Men'. (Joyce Agee, Catherine Elwes, Jacqueline Morreau, Pat Whiteread).

Another artist who was waging a campaign to show women's political art, though only by extension was it 'feminist', was the Austrian-born artist, Gertrude Elias. She put on two shows at the Swiss Cottage Library in 1977 and 1978 entitled 'The World as We See It', including work by Hilda Bernstein on the subject of apartheid.

The present writer was involved in a number of the above initiatives, and became part of a group which wished to bring women's political/feminist work before a wider public.

The exhibition which came out of the work of this group, 'Women's Images of Men', consisted of 100 works by artists and it toured throughout Great Britain, had unprecedented press coverage, broke attendance records, but above all raised hitherto ignored issues, the most contentious of which was: 'What does a woman see and think when she turns around and views her "old masters"?'

Our work achieved many of its aims, and above all proved that the theme shows could contextualise work from a woman's point of view so that each piece could relate to the others, and wherein there would be no way of misunderstanding the gender of the artist or the intention of the work.

'About Time', the companion exhibition to 'Woman's Images of Men', extended the areas of work beyond wall pieces. It involved performances, installation and video and it introduced a wide range of work by women in which they revealed their experience within a world codified by men.

Although there were two other exhibitions of women's work in the autumn of 1980, Lucy Lippard's 'Issue' show, Claire Smith's 'Eight Women, Artists', it is out of the issues raised in 'Women's Image of Men' and 'About Time' that 'Pandora's Box' arose.

In order to maintain the visibility gained by 'Women's Images of Men', the artists from that show met to discuss the next initiative. Some were in favour of an exhibition to be called 'Women's Images of Women', but others felt this to be too unspecific a topic. In order to set up a more challenging exhibition, the title 'Pandora's Box' was chosen to re-examine culturally accepted attitudes towards women as seen through traditional cliches, stories and myths. There could then be a distancing and a layering of meaning within allegorical themes.

Mouse Katz and Gill Calvert decided to narrow the theme down again to the actual myth of Pandora and its various interpretations in order to strengthen the impact of this exhibition. There have been, of course, voices raised in protest over a theme from myth.

As in 'Women's Images of Men', when the organisers were

1. In the Seventies, the Rothko scandal was revealed. By 1980, connections between private galleries, museums and art galleries were to be seen more clearly than ever (as were the efforts to rewrite art history) in the 'Art Now' show at the Royal Academy. This tendency had grown into an unashamed fact when the 'New Art' at the Tate opened in 1933. Although hotly denied officially, it was apparent that money was promoting and defining art in a way more blatant than ever. A new generation of heroic (male) artists was being created through media hype, gifts to galleries, sponsorship of block-buster shows – of artists unknown just yesterday. Schnabel, Bazeilitz etc.

   None of this is new, even after the First World War, Gertrude Stein tells us, that the art dealers were manipulating the art market in order to kill cubism. (Gertrude Stein, 1933, pg. 102) 'The Autobio-graphy of Alic B Toklas'). After the Second World War, the United States government was accused of 'cultural imperialism' the purpose of which was to kill off social realist art and drown it under the new abstract expressionism which was considered to be a more 'pure' art, without distressing content.

2. Painters like Rothko, Gottleib and Pollock fell back on the unlimited possibilities of myth and from communal myth and the primordial associations artists thought to evoke, it was a short step, taken almost immediately, to the personal myth. The unabashedly subjective invention of content. Dore Ashton 1957, 'An Eastern View of the San Fransisco School' in Evergreen Review: Vol 1, No. 2, 1957, Grove Press.

accused of 'wasting energy on men', so the present organisers were chastised for a 'sentimental descent into mythology'. When men had done this in the past, it was an area of 'unlimited possibilities'.

However, the exhibition easily avoids either 'sentiment' or neo-classicism. The work allows the viewer to take a leap of under-standing, and, since the many-layered myth allows for so many readings, the artist shows the way within the context, to her own interpretation.

There ought to have been a great many other women's shows between 1980 and 1984, but in fact there were few that attracted much public notice, though women gained much wider acceptance in the commercial sector and showed in small groups or singly in Arts Council galleries. 'Sense and Sensibility' in Nottingham was one group show in 1982. 'At the Crossroads' in 1981, during the Falklands War was an attempt to keep the artists from 'Women's Images of Men' together and commenting on current issues. From this writer's point of view, artists can and should engage in an evaluation of current issues in the world and make work which reveals new insights to a wide public. I believe we have demon-strated how this can be done effectively, especially through group shows. We hope that groups will continue to proliferate as they are doing all over the country. However, it is very clear that no matter how hard these groups work, and what they have to say, it is still extremely difficult to show these kind of alternative critiques in major galleries. Women are still an undersubsidised, undervalued group within the British art world. This, in spite of the fact that many men have told me, from some of the youngest arts admin-istrators to a venerable Cork Street dealer, that women are doing the only really interesting work these days.

What the Left has called for in the way of art intervention has not really appeared, what the theoreticians have wished to see did not work when artists have tried to put it into practice. Artists' desires to express ideas has sometime outstripped their 'techniques' and they have not created a new recognisable formal style. Therefore they are still suspect, but I believe that the idea that the 'medium is the message' has outlived its usefulness, and that we are seeing an era wherein the message must bring the medium best suited to it, with it.

Women have had only a moment's visibility in this century, but already the men are complaining. Money, authority, bureaucracy are being used to bury us. We have not had the long years of self-assurance in which we could indulge in normal heroics. But I am quite sure that we are the voice of our time, and must continue to try to bring female meanings into the public consciousness, as an alternative to the over-developed phallic quest for power, which will extinguish us all when it reaches its ultimate explosion.

MOUSE KATZ
Preparing Pandora

Why have another exhibition of Women's art? Indeed, why have art at all? At least a few people reading this must have pondered these questions from time to time: I certainly have. In *Beyond the Crisis in Art* Peter Fuller describes ours as a time when art is incomprehensible to all but an educated few, a time when 'no one wants fine artists except fine artists, and that neither they nor anyone else have the slightest idea what they should be doing, or for whom they should be doing it.' It does seem to me that many artists, dealers, buyers and the general public are floundering, waiting for the next big trend, or gimmick to set in; looking for some individual who will produce a new kind of work that is infinitely copiable.

Is art something to decorate the vaults of the elite, waiting for the moment when they may bring out their unique treasure, perhaps the culmination of another person's life's work, and exchange it for yet more of piles of paper money. Or is art something to hang in museums and force young children and art students to venerate as though immortals had left their imprint on these works while the number of copies, forgeries and inevitable restorations insure that few works of any age contain the presence of the famous signature at the bottom?

It is said that the best art is never appreciated in its own time. This leads to speculation on 'bad art' that no one likes in the expectation that it will miraculously become good art in time; and conversely fosters the conviction that the only good artist is a dead artist. This means that most contemporary artists have a very difficult time earning a living. Fictional poverty may be romantic, the reality is not. This has relevance not only to the personal lives of artists but to the fine arts in general. In the 1983 GLC report on the visual arts by Conrad Atkinson and Margaret Harrison, the authors state '. . . the market for visual artists in this country is very small and without a fundamental intervention to integrate the visual arts into the fabric of our public institutions the outlook is bleak.' The situation, bad for men is even worse for women. Their findings disclose that few visual artists earn a living wage from their work, and must pursue dual careers, 70% of these are engaged in teaching. However, even in the instance of pursueing a dual career, the average income for a visual artist are well below comparable professions. Those who earn over £15,000 number only 0.6%. An average wage for a male artist in the highest income group (age 55-64) is £8,364 for dual career. For woman the comparative figure drops to £2,532. For the relatively small group who are single career artists in the same age group, income drops to £4,320 per annum for men (£3,124 derived from bursaries and awards) and £1,514 for women of which only £133 comes from awards and bursaries. A small survey by Feminist Art News found that although the ratio of male to female art students was about equal, the numbers of full time staff were 69 males and 6 females, and in part time employment males out-

numbered females 48 to 19. The present government spends
£1,000 million on the Falklands compared with £100 million on the
arts, of which, as Sonia York points out that only 4½ million go to
the visual arts. She goes on to say of the Arts Council, 'they do
purchase a certain amount of work, it is true, and they do have
exhibitions, but nearly always of established artists. If little support
is given to the visual arts by the Arts Council, even less is given by
the media. The press record on treatment of these arts is distinctly
poor. Every week the better quality papers devote one or two
whole pages to books and daily there are several reviews of various
musical events. A medium quality musician will have several
reviews in a year, while one excellent artist, who has laboured for
two years on a new exhibition (for which the Arts Council 'rate of
pay' for a one-person exhibition in designated galleries is still only
£100), will be lucky to rate a small paragraph of art criticism.
Television and radio are as bad.' This is a personal view of one artist
(although shared by many) it is backed up by the GLC report on the
visual arts. 'It is worth pointing out however that newspaper critics
reporting on the visual arts in the main tend to concentrate on
those artists who show in private galleries (and even these have a
few artists who are able to live by selling work) and this sector
influences heavily the work which is shown in both public galleries
and exhibitions of English art abroad and this in turn influences
the art education and its priorities within our fine art departments.'
Of course, the majority of these few chosen artists are men.

These are but a few of the depressing facts on the visual arts.
Various solutions to these and other problems have been put
forward by informed and caring people. Many of these hinge upon
making contemporary visual art, and more particularly feminist
art more accessible and understandable to the general public. This
exhibition was conceived and developed as a response to this.

I cannot hope to speak for all women, anymore than this exhibition
can hope to represent all women. The 'feminine' is not exclusive to
the female gender, nor necessarily a large part of it. But, based
upon the above information, which conforms to classic conceptions
of 'masculine' and 'feminine', I would like to suggest a more
'feminine' view of what art might be.

Aesthetics and good taste apart, for these are things of fashion,
subject to personal whim and fancy, 'good' art has personal validity
and meaning for people. It may effect a change for the better in
your life, and give you new insights, be they intellectual, emotional
or spiritual – ideally all three. It may simply be a source of
physical/sensual pleasure that enables you to see in a new way, to
feel better in yourself. It is also a mirror of yourself, and will reflect
back what you are, or might become. In this sense, fine art has the
power to influence society, not only as inspiration for the design of
various consumer products, but on a deeper level because the fine
arts are associated with what Jung refers to as symbols of the

psyche. Our visual perceptions infiltrate our unconscious and become the means by which we shape reality. If we do not give proper regard to those influences that shape our destiny, we are, without doubt, choosing to abandon control of ourselves into the hands of others. For this reason, it is important to know the source from which images spring and to look at art through the eyes of a child, not with naivety, but with an openness and purity untainted by the expectations of outside authority.

In discussing the evils inherent in conformity and stereotyping, Carl Rodgers states 'Unless man can make new and original adaptations to his environment as rapidly as his science can change the environment, our culture will perish. Not only individual maladjustment and group tensions, but international annihilation will be the price we pay for lack of creativity'. With the rise of computer technology and the decline of religion and other forms of dogmatic guidance, art will become more important as a means of stimulating the growth of individual consciousness, and thereby the further development of our civilization. The fine arts, as well as being the final product of the creativity of a small group of individuals, also serve to arouse creativity in others. But in a world where the majority of art comes from the male, where is the woman to look for images and symbols that are meaningful to her? Equally, how is man to understand the female if he persists in using the experience of other men as his only or major reference?

Much of the problematical side of feminism is taken up with the desire to define 'woman' as she really is. In the art world, many believe that all-women exhibitions, such as this are necessary, not only to redress the balance of women's exclusion from the fine arts, but also as a means of allowing women the freedom to be what ever she is, without distortion by any process of defensiveness, or competitiveness with men. It should give women the opportunity to try out concepts, beliefs, perceptions and hypotheses, in a supportive and relatively non-judgemental atmosphere. My experience of women artists over the years is that their self confidence grows in proportion to the decrease in the anxiety of separateness; the realization that she is not 'alone' leads to increased integrity in her art and in turn spurs her on to a greater desire to communicate her experience to others.

I cannot agree with those who fear that this type of experience will lead women into an artistic ghetto, from which they will not be able to escape, I believe it is more likely to confer an independence that will allow women to enter the 'art world' in their own right. It also allows women (artists) to be seen in another context. In *The Sceptical Feminist*, Janet Radcliffe Richards says '. . . no single environment can show the nature of anything, because to know the nature of anything (a woman . . .) is to know its potential; that if it is in one environment it will behave in one way; that if it is in another, it may be different. The reason we do not know about the nature of women, and of course men, is not that we have seen them in the wrong environments, but that we have not seen them in enough different ones.'

In 1980 approximately 20 artists, participants in "Womens Images of Men" (ICA 1980) met to discuss the results and ramifications of that show. It had been very popular, the attendance in each of the 6 venues was at least ⅓ above normal. It was said the ICA had not seen so many people since Andy Warhol a decade earlier. Friendships had developed amongst the artists and a small support network had begun. We felt we couldn't go back and another exhibition was needed to sustain what had begun. I *thought* it would be a quick and easy task, 6 months at the most, simply letting all the artists and venues know that there would be another Women's Images show. I naively thought that one success would deserve another chance. A year later, we had not been able to interest any London venue in the show.

The artists were chosen from open submission publicized in the art press, womens magazines and newspapers, local and national. The method of selection was unorthodox. It was a long, slow almost organic process. We spent nearly 2 years looking at the work of hundreds of women artists, and evolving the criteria that we would use in selecting the work. Each of us were totally different in our outlook, but all agreed that we were looking for work that "spoke" to us on an emotional, intellectual and spiritual level. We looked for women with ideas as well as a command of media and techincal skill. The work might be in any medium or genre within the representational range. We tried to understand the attributes that might make a work specifically female. We wanted a wide selection of work, serious and with humour, that would be accessible to the general pubic and have an effect beyond the immediate exhibition. I tried particularly to look for potential in women who seemed only to lack the confidence a show like this might bring. After many arguments about quality, standards and the meaning of life, we asked 100 artists to submit further work on the theme. The work that arrived was exciting, mystifying, disappointing. Many artists had changed their work considerably in the intervening period, for better or worse. A few never replied and one simply passed on her selection notice to a friend. By this time I had contacted Lewis Biggs who was then the exhibitions director at the Arnolfini. He was excited by the idea of the show and agreed to take it on and give whatever help he could. We were given a small grant by GLAA, but still could not find a London venue. Due to the size of the show we were limited to choice, but approached 5 public galleries. One was closing for renovations, two just said no, one said no because it didn't wish to be seen putting on a bunch of womens shows and one explained that their policy was to only take mixed shows . . . although we have actually seen very few women exhibited there. It seemed as though we were trying to resusitate a dead raccoon, but remained determined, believing that it was an essential thing to do.

Then somehow the tide seemed to turn, friends came and regional galleries became interested in the show, the Arts Council gave us a grant and Jill Morgan offered us the services of Rochdale gallery as an organizing venue. Jill had a lot of enthusiasm for the show and strong interests in the general state of women's art. We formed a final selection committee consisting of Jill Morgan, Bev Bytheway, Lewis Biggs, Gill Calvert and myself.

The 32 final artists were selected with great difficulty. During the long selection process, Gill and I talked with them, visited them, or saw their work, tried to be as supportive and positive as possible, knowing that not everyone could be in the show. Many of the women seemed to have difficulties of one kind or another, Bernadette O'Donohue says 'one explanation could have been the actual length of time the idea of the project covered . . . with such a long·time to work on the theme, I think many women lost their original ideas, and new ones brought about by further research became too difficult to interpret, and in turn making the artist feel uncertain as to what her original expectations were.' For myself and Gill Calvert, this was particularly true. Because we were organizing the exhibition we had very little time left for our own work, but more pertinently, we were constantly bombarded by the added stimulation of talking to and seeing the work of the other artists.

In retrospect, I believe that the years of hard work were very worthwhile, not only in terms of the final product, but in the learning experience as artists and organizers, I hope that we will inspire others to do the same, in order to create a tradition of Women's Images exhibitions.

In putting together this catalogue, we tried to remain faithful to the basic ideals of the show. Because we wish to reach the wider 'non art' public as well as other artists and afficionados, we have tried to avoid 'art language', the statements are conversational in tone. They are for the most part exactly as the artists wrote them, so that they might be a reflection of their personality rather than an editors sleight of hand. Some of the artists are practiced in the art of writing; but for most it was a difficult task to put their thoughts and feelings not only into words, but into print. They speak of their lives, their work, many of the issues now being confronted in the womens art movement. We hope that this catalogue may give the reader a better understanding of the works in this exhibition and the women who made them. We believe it is important, if we are to effect the overall creative maturity of womankind, to foster an environment in which the individual woman feels safe to express her uniqueness in words and images. In like manner, we welcome your comments, criticisms, and commendations.

Mouse Katz
on behalf of myself and Gill Calvert

Jaqueline Morreau
Within the Apple, Eve and Adam
Oil on board, 39 x 33 ins.

Allison Allnutt
"I say fellows . . ."

Katya Coupland
Exploding Handbag
Oil on canvas

Penny Woolcock
"Dressed in glittering raiment they drank heavily,
laughing loudly"
Oil, felt-tip, acrylic, 132 x 96 ins.

Works & Statements

Sonia York

Sonia York

Although women are working under considerable difficulties, both financial and domestic, there are some very exciting developments taking place in women's art. There are so many talented women working today, that solid foundations are being laid for a new self-confidence among women artists. The women's movement, which some have condemned for being over-agressive, has now begun to achieve what it set out to do. *Women are working with a new conviction; they are now no longer saying 'I am a woman' but more importantly 'I am an artist.'*

My First Pandora's Painting Book
Watercolour

THE THEME OF PANDORA'S BOX
The theme of 'Pandora's Box' seemed on first sight a limiting subject. On further thought, however, greater possibilities appeared and the more interesting it appeared as a theme.

Although guilt was the first thought that occurred on the subject, it then seemed that more important issues were involved. A different interpretation of the story could be that it is another version of the story of Adam and Eve.

Both Pandora and Eve are tempted, both give into temptation and with the knowledge of evil the innocence of both is destroyed. The loss of innocence seems one of the most important

issues today.
Children seem, in our 'you can have it all' society, to be encouraged to smoke, drink, take drugs and have sex before they are mature enough to cope with the consequences. They are threatened with war and the bomb before they are out of their cradles and are encouraged to fight for their rights as though other people's rights had a lower value. Children need time to become civilised adults, a time of peace and innocence.

This idea was important to me, but could I find a way of representing it clearly enough for everyone to understand it? It occurred to me that this problem could be solved through the medium of something closely associated with children.

One thought was an obvious one to any painter – a painting-book. So the idea for *My First Pandora Painting Book* was formed. I wanted the cover to look both innocent and authentic; so chose to use the style of Mabel Lucie Attwell and similar artists, who were working during my childhood. Although I have done an imaginary painting, it is how I feel she might have done it. When the viewer opens the book, as I hope she or he will, what are they expecting? I hope the scene revealed will give the viewer a slight shock. This is what the world must seem like to an innocent child — full of shocks, possibly only half–understood at first, but, with constant repetition, soon understood only too well.

Continuing with this theme, I next painted *Tiny Tots Sewing Kit*, subtitled *The Battering of the World*. It is obviously unsuitable for tiny tots to sew, (a despairing woman in sewing card form) it is a glimpse of the horrors of the world, which affect children.

As I was finishing the sewing kit, there were in *The Sunday Times*, some most unpleasant photographs of dead elephants. Although young children rarely read the newspapers, it must be remembered, that even tiny children look at the photos in the colour supplements. To bring home this destruction of innocence, I first

thought of a horrifying picture of Winnie-the-Pooh and Christopher Robin, as the epitome of good and innocent characters, cutting up some dead elephants. This idea seemed sick, but not as sick as the photographs. I then toned down the whole idea, with a painting of these characters merely thinking of the idea. The title is *Horror Story*.

There are many ways children are forced into early maturity. I point out further examples in *Happy Families Reader Book I*. This is a school-type reading-book with a difference. At first glance all seems sweetness and light. There are lists of 'new words' on each five-line page, and I have kept to the exact format this type of book would

Destruction of innocence
Colour Supplement
Watercolour, 11.5 x 9 ins.

have. Although *Happy Families* is the title and the first page begins with Mother and Dad and the children going to school, things soon start to go a little sour. Mother and Dad, like so many Mothers and Dads, do not behave as they should. As the book progresses they behave worse and worse. The culmination in tragedy on the last page is optional, as many people prefer to stop with a semblance of happiness on the page before. The book embodies some of the truths of life, which children have to face in the adult world.

Although these paintings are quite different from my usual style, I have

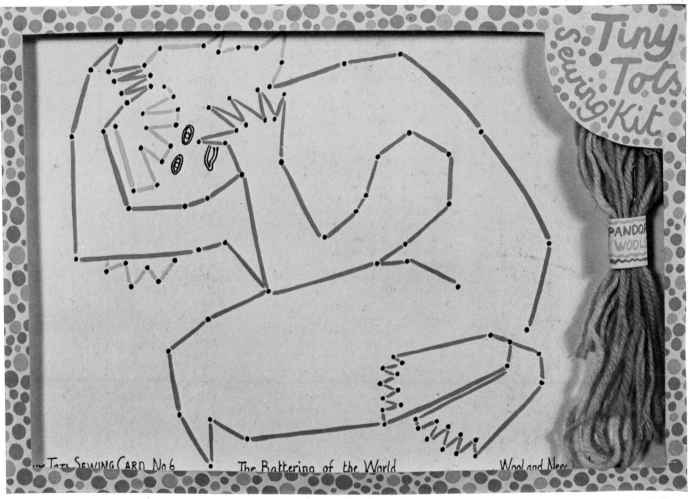

Tiny Tots Sewing Kit
Gouache, needle and wool, 7 x 10 ins.

found the stimulation of ideas generated by 'Pandora's Box' fascinating and am continuing with further work in this direction.

AN AUTOBIOGRAPHICAL NOTE
I have painted and drawn since childhood, but like so many women, there have been long pauses in my artistic life. Marriage at nineteen in 1960 interrupted art education and children a little later put a stop to serious work. It was not until ten years after that that I began to prepare for a first exhibition, though I had exhibited in local mixed exhibitions in the meantime. Living in an isolated house in the country with husband and children out all day, the loneliness then became too much and I worked as a garden designer for seven years. I returned to serious art when the need to paint became overwhelming and in 1981 started to work for a first exhibition in London. Since then I have been exhibiting in many different mixed exhibitions, both in East Anglia and London. I am planning an exhibition at the Minories in Colchester in early 1985.

I most enjoy painting people; people who are totally self-absorbed, thinking only of what they are doing and unaware of a spectator. My paintings, although usually based on life are painted from memory, or entirely from imagination. I like to think about them for a long time before actually putting anything on paper.

Art is really more important as a means of promoting happiness than of wallowing in despair. Art is for giving pleasure. Like writing and music, art is a gift from the artist to the world and such generosity should not be spurned.

Sonia York

Lois Williams

"Whoosh!"
Wood, card and paint, cart 13 x 11 x 10 ins.

Boxes are a common feature of our daily lives and almost all of us make use of them. Quite simply they are containers – often perishable, sometimes fashionable, occasionally decorative – used primarily to keep and protect objects or personal possessions from damage. Most of our gifts and presents are packed in boxes, and according to Hesiod, Pandora was 'the first woman upon whom the gods lavished their choicest gifts. Though forbidden to do so, she opened a box containing all human ills and allowed these to escape, but managed to save the good gift of 'Hope'. I have consistently used the image of the box/container over a number of years in a number of different ways: to produce work on the theme seemed a natural extension of the work I was doing.

The use and choice of materials is an important aspect of my work. It is in the selection of a specific material that governs the structure and content of the work to varying degrees. The materials used are readily accessible – wool, sacking, twine, wood, paper –

their qualities are all important and an integral concern. Some pieces relate to domestic imagery, alluding to objects which are clothed, enwrapped, hidden: household objects, personal possessions , keepsakes. Other pieces are almost completely concerned with the process of making – woven paper, sewn sacking, papier maché structures. Virtually no tools are involved, the main emphasis lies in the close contact with the material and its transformation. This response to materials and their manipulation is an immediate way could be said to be favoured by women.

Currently I teach in Sheffield whilst at the same time maintaining strong links with my home in North Wales. My studio spaces are vastly different: one is an attic room in a large house in a Sheffield suburb (small, well lit and warm) the other is an old Welsh long house with no electricity, no amenities, and sheep walking past the window. While studying Fine Art at Manchester Polytechnic, the course was structured in such a way as to allow me to develop my own methods of working. These methods are everchanging and travelling from an urban space to an open rural environment has helped to stimulate new work. A situation which at first hand seemed to be a disadvantage has in fact proved productive.

Over a number of months I have worked intermittently on the theme of 'Pandora's Box' and several three-dimensional pieces have resulted. All in mixed media, their scale is small, their surfaces shabby and unpolished, their nature intimate. A feature common to each piece has been the subdivision of the main spatial area into many chambers like tombs or vaults.

The Black Garden is a completely enclosed structure with no apparent lid: its many compartments are held tightly together to protect its inner secrets. Colour is used simply – wool, clay slip – and its exterior is unadorned. This simplicity is echoed in another piece *Whoosh!* Here I have used the most basic of all carrying

devices – the cart. Living on a farm has been particularly influential, providing a rich source for material and imagery. This piece is strongly reminiscent of the sometimes crude vehicles used by farmers. Its fractured structures move along unsteadily, some filled, some empty, nothing can be prevented from escaping. A cart to suit all needs?

Over the past few years I have taught full-time in a comprehensive school, making an effort to visit my studio space each day. Its easy accessibility has meant that I am able to set time aside to develop work, to consider new ideas and maintain continuity. Although much of the work is made in isolation I find it particularly stimulating and supportive to participate in a group exhibition such as this.

Looking through
Wood, paper, glass and scrim, 16 x 20 x 5.5 ins.

Lois Williams

Bernadette O'Donohue

I was born on 4th August 1958, studied at Ravensbourne College of Art, (1978) and Wolverhampton Polytechnic, (1979-1982) where I was a print option student on a Graphic Design Course. Since leaving college I have continued to make my own work which consists of collages and boxes, whilst coming to terms with the difficulties that face many art students upon leaving college.

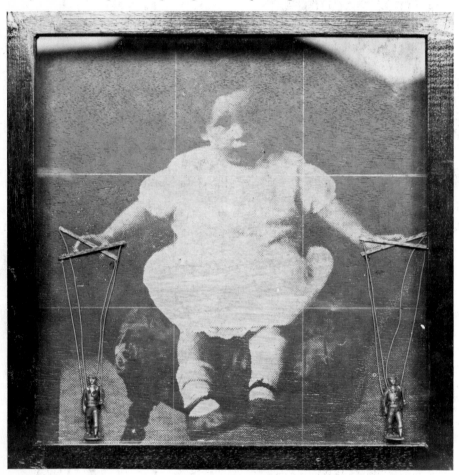

Pandora's Box 3: The Myth
Screen-print on plywood

I had my first two-man exhibition in October 1983, which was held at Woodlands Art Gallery, Blackheath. Prior to that I exhibited in the Printmakers Council's, 'Across the Frontiers' and the Humberside 2nd Printmaking Competition, 1982. I have recently been offered a studio with Space Studios in Deptford and with this space I hope to develop my collages and boxes.

My first major piece of work after leaving college was my work on 'Pandora's Box'. This work proved to be a challenge in many ways, especially since it wasn't my own personal work brief, for the brief was set by a group of women artists for the purpose of expressing women artists' views on a subject matter that had strong associations with society and how its prejudices and fears were related to women.

My first approach to answering the brief was to read as many books as possible on the subject but the more reading I did, the more prejudiced and confused I became, for I was constantly aware that my feelings could be swayed by the feminist bias I associated with Women's Images. It was important that I portrayed my own feelings on the subject and not those that I thought might be expected of me. **Eventually after much time thinking the subject and little to prove creatively I chose to portray Pandora's Box as a myth created by men as an excuse for all the wrong they had done and as a result blaming women and making them innocent victims of man's own creation.**

When thinking about making an image I thought the box as a container was too obvious, but a box with all sides laid open as in an open plan had more connotations: it becomes symbolic of a crucifix and with it associations of death and victory. My first box was to show the death and sufferings associated with it.

Pandora's Box 1 – A child of yesterday.

In this piece I portrayed Pandora as a child of 1914, an innocent victim, a minder of all those people killed as a result of the First World War. The middle square contains a circle which symbolises the poppy and with it a reminder of those many bare wooden crosses that are scattered throughout France. To produce the image I had a photographic halftone made from an original photograph and then screen-painted the halftone onto plywood. I then cut the squares out, hinged the bottom square to represent the box lid, painted the circle and then aged the wood slightly before glueing onto a back support.

My second piece of work was made as a result of talking to one of the women organisers who suggested I made a further piece to represent the women of today. In making this piece I thought of the women of Greenham Common, and their attempts to make people aware of the dangers that nuclear weapons can have upon our society, with this in mind I produced *Pandora's Box 2 'A Woman of our time'.*

In this piece my aim was to show the hope that can come from within the box. This time the crucifix shape of the open box symbolizes victory rather than death. For this piece I took a photograph of my sister and had a photo halftone made which I then screenprinted onto plywood. I then cut the cross shape out and also the circle her hands were clasping. Inside the circle I laid a round piece of glass to create the feeling that she was looking into a crystal ball and a future in which she has a strong role to play.

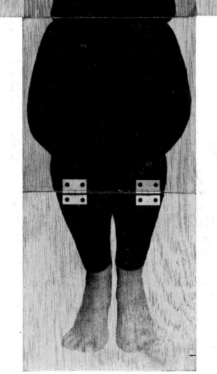

I made my third piece of work to represent the stereotype image that many have of Pandora. This piece is called *Pandora's Box 3 – The Myth*.

In this piece I have again used the image of the little girl but this time she represents evil not innocence. She sits within a square, in either hand a soldier puppet, signs of her manipulative powers over men's fate.

As a result of working on the theme of Pandora's Box with Women's Images, I was made aware not only of the many difficulties that had faced the women organisers in trying to get support for a touring exhibition but also the difficulties some women had encountered when answering the brief. I had imagined myself the only woman

artist to have difficulties translating my thoughts into images and on discovering that others had also had problems, I wondered why this had arisen.

Whilst working on the project I also became aware of a common problem that affects many women artists – that of isolation. Until this project I hadn't had any contact with other women artists. This I feel is very important, for by doing so we can encourage each

Pandora's Box: A Woman of our time
Screen-print on plywood

other to break away from the barriers that we create in our heads. I think being a woman artist is very difficult because we have to come to terms with our expected roles of mother and wife and learn how to make a compromise. But such problems should help to make us stronger in the end.

As much as I enjoy a good painting or piece of sculpture so I enjoy work that makes demands upon its viewer mentally or physically. My own approach to work is to produce images that make people think and to create a subtle twist. I will develop this approach with time and a better understanding of both myself and my work.

Bernadette O'Donohue

Pascale Petit

Born in Paris in 1953, I took my degree in sculpture at Gloucestershire College of Art. From 1978-81, I worked as a freelance designer, making exotic headwear, to buy my sculpture materials. In 1980 I held a two-woman exhibition in the New Gallery, Hornsey Library. My sculptures from the exhibition were featured in the Womans Page of the Guardian, and photos and prose excerpts published in Ad Astra. I am a writer and my sculpture has a literary base. I have had poems published in numerous poetry magazines, and have given readings in many venues around the country and in London, including at Angels of Fire festivals. I am working towards a first collection of poems. A novel 'The May Queen' was written at the same time as 'Ancestral Memory', and one from enriched the other. I wrote the novel **over four years, guided by seasonal changes from winter to spring. The** May Queen is the Snow Queen's successor. The glass sculpture took two years to evolve.

Pandora's Box for me means the power of the female, which has been pushed into the unconscious by men, throughout history. The box is the womb and the brain, both storage places of the human past – in the brain it is stored in the unconscious and memory, in the womb through the development of the embryo. I am obsessed by birth and wombs because of personal experience. I was a premature baby placed in an incubator (hence the glass and translucent materials) and my mother almost died giving birth to me. Then I was not brought up by her so the 'mother' became a distant alien person for me. Most of my interest in sculpture materials is in varying degrees of translucency, and 'not-there-ness'. My experience has made me sensitive to the universal problem of the 'not-there-ness' of female consciousness, which has been pushed into the unconscious where it becomes negative and wreaks havoc – the 'Terrible Mother'. The benevolent mother is personified, I think, in the Greenham Common women.

In art we can see that there has been no feminie consciousness – all the history of art is male. Any feminine art that has been produced, has been done by men. There is therefore, half of the world population's life-experience that has been denied expression. I find male work alien because it is foreign to me – there were no father-figures in my family.

My work deals with female experience – birth, change, women and their alienation from the male dominated world, and their subsequent roles of invisibility. In 'Mirror' the first woman – Pandora or Eve – sees herself in the reflection man provides. What she sees is her twin – the unconscious – where the objects (which are dad or inert) are more visible than her flesh. The woman looking at herself is translucent, has not become a fully-formed female entity, but a glass woman, passive receptacle for men's wills, not the mature female counterpart to men. Mirrors are a recurrent theme and image in my novel *The May Queen* where the main character sees reflections of her unconscious self in mirrors. Here is an excerpt from the chapter 'Mirror':

'Anna was still drifting on the brink of consciousness. The glass was cracking. Her face was dividing into finer and finer stitches, a criss-cross of cuts and sub-divisions. A thread of glass unwound from the mirror like the web a spider spins. Her face was unravelling. The mirror changed from a two-dimensional surface into a sphere. She used the unwinding ball as a clew and ventured into the palace. By now she knew its myriad halls and many of its labyrinthine corridors, so she found her way through them, seeking its heart.

The ball of glass kept on unravelling as she walked forward. She always knew it had been a magic ball which would change its shape along the way. When she reached the innermost chamber Anna went in, glancing quickly behind her to see if a

single thread of glass would show her the way back.

Reclining at the centre of her pool of mirrors was the Snow Queen. Her gowns shone like starlight and her eyes flashed diamonds. She was busy re-arranging her blocks of reason; a game she had devised to pass away time, for she was immortal'.

Mirror
Mixed media (unfinished)

I have many of my own guesses as to what I was making in 'Ancestral Memory' – I'll suggest a few – though I hope that it suggests different things to other people: for me it could be a glass womb or incubator, or a glass brain with its right and left hand sides, it's about being and nothingness, is Sleeping Beauty's palace, where the unborn potential of the feminine waits, it could be about the world-balance; Antarctica versus rainforests. It is also about sanity – the brittle nature of its material might suggest this. The birds were once dinosaurs. In this sculpture humans are only photo remnants. I have noticed that neutron bombs destroy people, but not photographs. Although it's almost invisible, 'not-there', glass is dangerous. All kinds of palaces appear in my novel. Here is an excerpt from the chapter called 'The Palace of Light':
'Its thick stone walls reflect the

midday sun in unparalleled brilliance. It is so white that it is painful to the eyes, burns them. It emits a white heat, scorches to the touch. It is a holy palace, abode of ancestor spirits. On the inside there is the dark of a grave. There spirits huddle around the pillars and cupolas, shielded from the piercing sun, which would turn them to vapour.

This is also the palace that Anna inhabits, but as she crosses its threshold the gloom is dispersed and the rooms fill with light and air. The retreating voices evaporate. Now if she glances out of the windows she sees a pitch black night. It's as if she wields enough power to reverse the order of things.

Anna was standing in the great hall surveying her reflection in the mirror. Its surface clouded over into a mist. It darkened, then she knew that it was a window to the exterior of the palace. At first she thought that the luminous disc in the sky was the moon, but looking harder she realised that it was a primitive type of clock, hanging in the dark.

Below the clock, in a clearing of the primeval forest, she saw twelve slabs of stone arranged in a circle. About the stones moved a figure. It occured to her that one of the ancestral spirits had escaped from the walls and was now wandering out in the open. The figure had a look of one distracted, as if it had been driven from its rightful place. Suddenly it darted forward, and as it passed by, she recognised Juliette.

Juliette ran on for miles. She had been out walking in the grounds of the hospital, which overlooked the palace. She had looked up, and to her alarm, had seen the palace pulsating with radiant light. The brilliance had almost blinded her and she ran off to hide herself from its

Detail of 'Mirror'

glare. Passing by the perimeters of the great hall, she had caught sight of Anna standing at the window. She too had glowed with unnatural light.'

When I work I have lots of ideas. If one particular idea persists for long enough I will plan how to make it. Then there is a long period of technical work, which modifies and develops the original idea, and the result is where the idea meets the possibilities of the materials. Usually I am disappointed with the results, but this spurs me on to try again, rethinking the technique. Most work I do is slow, partly because of financial difficulties, and lack of space, partly because it is an organic process that needs to grow steadily, so that I feel the end result has depth and many layers of meaning.

I don't know if there are differences between men and women's technical approaches – but I do know that the content of my sculpture is female, and therefore different from a man's. I can't speak for other women – many follow in the steps of male tradition, as this is where the standards of excellence are set.

I have always been single-minded and followed my own vision. All of my work has dealt with the condition of being human – the opposite of male phallic art – about owning a receptacle with the power of life and death, pleasure and pain – the pain of childbirth, periods, the pleasure of sex. While saying this, I am also aware that men have a contemptuous attitude towards female genitals. Recently I watched a television dramatisation of an operation where the surgeons were cutting 'the box'

out as if it was an inferior organ. I realise that this attitude is mixed with fear of the unknown.

As regards the art establishment, I have always felt that my art was different, and don't like sculptures about sculptures. When I first heard about Womens Images' plans I felt for the first time that there might be others like me, that I was not an alien, alone. This was mainly because of the mythological and literary theme of the show, and its premise that work should be about women, which gave me a feeling of kinship. Also, thre being artists of many nationalities, as I have always felt European influences on me rather than British.

As for my experience of art college – on my foundation course I was mocked for doing work about literary themes. My experience on my degree course was happier – the sculpture department being fairly free. In retrospect, the fact that the tutors were all men seems a drawback – though this was partly my fault, at twenty I had no idea how to cope with or even recognise sexism. Of course I feel discrimination as a woman artist. It's harder to exhibit and get Arts Council awards.

I think there are areas of experience that women are more able to describe – such as birth, change, the passage of time – women being more in touch with nature biologically. We're particularly able to describe the unconscious, because we're so familiar with it, it being where most of us hide. I suspect (though I'm not sure) that women prefer to depict the cruel and ephemeral quality of time, making sculptures that break easily, rather than the eternal monuments that defy time's ravages, that have been made by men in the past; are more likely to produce organic art, than formal and geometric, but I acknowledge that men and women are both a mixture of genders, so I'm not suggesting that only men make male art – it's more a case of feminie and masculine art. Surely it's time that women created more of the feminine art around, and time for Beauty to awake before the palace breaks?

Pascale Petit

Jacqueline Morreau

Jacqueline Morreau

WOMEN AND MYTHOLOGY

How can we show hidden aspects of the familiar? How can we present the unfamiliar so that it can be recognized? We all transform reality into new meanings in our dreams. We wake full of fear, wonder, longing, and perhaps new insight. Dreams, myths, fairy tales, legends, even jokes, present familiar ideas in an unfamiliar way.

I have always dealt with dream material and metaphor (that is, one thing standing for another) in my work. At first I did this unconsciously and, inevitably, with unconscious additions. In an early etching, for instance, I had depicted a family group full of tension. I could not put an ear onto the head of the father. I thought it 'spoiled the composition'. I reworked it several times, and still no ear. Not only my literally deaf father, but all the men who will not listen, made that absence essential to the deeper meaning of the picture.

THE GREEKS

Greek mythology has been called 'an activity of the psyche externalised in images'[1] and also 'an unsurpassably spontaneous documentation of human nature.'[2] If you add to this that in mythology woman was on the throne not in the home, this literature is a most obvious source of material for the woman artist.

What also appeals to me is that this literature was not born out of fantasy alone. The Greeks were rational, and they believed in a rational world. They observed nature more closely than perhaps anyone before or since. But they never copied it, through their feeling for, and belief in Measure, Balance, and Necessity, they tried to reach the 'inner simplifying reality'[3] in all their arts.

USING MYTHOLOGY

Artists today can use mythological sources, and like the Greeks themselves, translate them into an 'inner simplifying reality', clothed so that they are meaningful for us today. If I as a woman can use them to give women's experience some reality for others, then I can be part of a

She Who Spins
Oil on board, 33 x 39 ins.

movement to bring meaning back into the visual arts. Of course the 'subject' is still only half the artist's job. The other half is to make everything else in the picture enhance the meaning on the visual and emotional level.

We can use not only myths but dreams, slogans, parables even puns for our own purposes and these will perhaps convey to the viewer some of the multiple meanings which we have worked out, and enjoyed making visible.

It is Pandora's curiosity which is blamed in the prevailing version of the myth, for bringing evil into the world. Eve is in every way Pandora's counterpart in our own culture.

Pandora/Eve is seen to have been sent by the Gods or God to defy a divine injunction. This seems hardly to make sense. It seems more logical to me that she was sent to obey a divine instruction.

Woman is chosen, rather than man, to obey this instruction, because it is through her that the new life is born, therefore it is through her that the new life of the race should be born.

Man cannot bring forth new life, he must wait for the woman to share it with him if she will.

If we take the myth as conveying a truth more profound than that of the male projection of his guilt onto the female, then her 'sin' was no sin at all, but the act which projected mankind into a new period wherein the simple life such as animals live was left behind forever, and the 'tragic choice between knowledge and contentment'[4] was, of necessity, made.

Pandora's Box can therefore be seen as her womb, out of which comes the human race, bearing, now, knowledge of good and evil, no longer merely creatures of instinct.

SHE WHO SPINS

The painting *She Who Spins* reflects my thoughts on Pandora's womb as the 'Box'. I have worked on the idea of the first of the three Fates, the one who spins, (her sisters are the one who weaves and the one who cuts the thread of life), the Mother Spinner, the spider, weaving out of her own body the web of life. The spider is a symbol common within our experience. It is not necessary to go back to the mythological source to be able to understand and feel some of the meanings I am trying to express. She symbolizes fecundity, she makes a web which is beautiful for some and dangerous for others, she symbolizes eternity, she symbolizes death. Birth implies the journey towards death, and so she who brings life brings also the promise of death.

PANDORA AS ATLAS

Another way of looking at the 'Box' was as woman's burden.

Marisa Rueda suggested to me the idea of Pandora as Atlas, holding up the world full of troubles on her shoulders. This idea developed into the painting where Earth herself is cracked and bleeding and full of sores. Pandora has still to carry it on her back like an ugly growth.

Perhaps we attach blame to Pandora for bringing us this terrible burden of choice. But the point is that we can choose. We do not have to choose those things which disturb the balance of nature such as atomic fission, genetic engineering, or bizarre medical practices which represent curiousity without morality. Out of the woman's movement may come the answer. The peace movement is part of a growing concern for our relationship to nature. Women's mysteries were all about cycles of birth, reproduction and death. Without respect for these cycles as inevitable, we have taken our ability to choose too literally. We are guilty of hubris, the sin of pride which the fates inevitably

Pandora as Atlas, 1983
Oil on canvas, 40 x 30 ins.

punish. Can women restore the balance?

Footnotes.

1. Kerényi, C., 1982, *The Gods of the Greeks*, Thames and Hudson, introduction pg. 3.

2. *Ibid*, pg. 2.

3. Kitto, H.D., 1957, *The Greeks*, Penguin, pg. 182.

4. Panofsky, Dora and Erwin, *Pandora's Box*, the changing aspect of a mythical symbol, 1962 (paperback, 1978) Princeton Bollingen Series LII. pg. 8 discussion of Babrius' version of the myth.

Jacqueline Moreau

Alison Allnutt

A theme for an exhibition helps to focus one's thoughts and ideas. It also gives a group exhibition coherence and a sense of purpose.

When the theme is as multi-faceted as 'Pandora's Box' there is no shortage of inspirational sources.

Contrary to popular belief, an artist often welcomes constraints and a structured framework within which to express ideas. Sydney Nolan, the famous Australian painter, in an interview with Richard Baker, said that he welcomed the challenge of designing sets for Wagner's 'Ring' cycle of operas and didn't mind in the least being 'told what to do.'

A sense of purpose and direction is most important, especially for artists working in isolation from other artists. Women artists, more often than men artists, work at home with little contact with other creative people. In this isolated situation it is easy to feel that there is no point in producing work. Motivation to work thrives on the stimulation, feedback and exchange of ideas from contact with other artists. **The role of Pandora in the myth of Pandora's Box is one of scapegoat. She acts more out of thoughtlessness and curiousity than malice – rather bland, negative characteristics which lack the passionate conviction of anger, revenge and overwhelming pride. Pandora's sins are trivial compared to Lucifer's. She is the mere agent through which Zeus revenges himself on mankind.** Positive, vengeful females are rare in history and literature. Boudicca, Joan of Arc and Charlotte Corday are famous because they acted in a startlingly unfeminine way.

That Pandora *will* open the Box is inevitable – she has been endowed with the stereotyped female personality traits of curiousity and impulsiveness. Therefore, the archetypal female, Pandora, is condemned for *being female* and having 'female' behaviour patterns and characteristics which are seen as being bad and leading to disastrous consequences.

The opening of the box by Pandora is surely a metaphor for the evil consequences of male enslavement to female sexuality – if men are seduced by female charms they will suffer the consequences.

The myth of Pandora's Box in Greek mythology has its Biblical equivalent in Adam and Eve's loss of paradise as a consequence of their disobedience in eating the forbidden fruit. Again, Eve is seen as the scapegoat. It was she who first succumbed to the serpent's temptation and caused not only her own downfall and Adam's but the whole of the human race. It is through Eve that mankind inherits original sin and a predisposition for evil, according to orthodox Christian doctrine.

Both Pandora and Eve are portrayed as young and beautiful; it is their sexuality that is seen as potentially threatening to male power. If men are to remain dominant they must keep women submissive subservient and above all control them, and thus harmless.

Looking through the names of the exhibitors in 1983's Northern Young Contemporaries Exhibition I noticed that at least fifty percent were female. In five or ten years time it is probable that fewer of the women than men will still be producing work on a regular basis. It is not difficult to suggest reasons for women artist's continuing 'low profile' in the fine arts. More empirical research is needed but I think the main problems faced by women artists could be described under the following headings: workspace and lack of contact with other artists.

Of course, men artists suffer from lack of money, studio-space and isolation but I believe women have problems in these areas to a greater degree. Firstly, financial backing – it requires a great deal of self confidence and a strong belief in the value of one's work to spend money on materials for painting, sculpture etc. It is hard to buy a tube of cadmium red when one needs a tube of tomato puree. Most women feel guilty buying fabric to make a collage or a wall-hanging when sheets are needed for a child's bed. This is especially true of women who have no paid employment.

Usually one can compromise, and there is no reason why good work should not be produced with limited materials and money but apart from the cost of materials there is the cost of framing or mounting and of transporting work to and from exhibitions. It is self-evident that the more avant-garde or non-commercial the work is, the less money will be made, and so the net result is a loss – hard to justify unless one is independent.

Lack of work space is another problem for many women artists. Again, one can compromise. A friend of mine who was the best painter of her year at the Royal Academy School found that it was more convenient to make fabric wall hangings which could be done a bit at a time and rolled up out of the way of ubiquitous toddlers. The resulting work was exciting and original and was shown at the prestigious John Moore's exhibition.

Often the limited work space available limits the size and scale of work which can be produced.

A male artist I know has recently completed a 14 ft. high painting – hardly possible in the kitchen. Because the space used by a woman artist is often used for other purposes she has to work in an episodic, disjointed way

Women's lives tend to be punctuated by other peoples needs and demands. There are no long, uninterrupted periods when one's work can evolve. Work is sporadic – the woman artist tends to lose track of her ideas and to lose interest in them before they can be developed.

I have often come across ideas for projects which I have scribbled on the back of envelopes, or scraps of paper – not because they were bad or impracticable but because some other task had intervened. It is male artists who have the chance to produce long series of work on one topic or theme that intrigues them.

Perhaps the most detrimental factor affecting women artists after they leave college is isolation from other artists. There is no feedback, no interchange of ideas, no criticism and no encouragement. One has to be very high motivated to work in a vacuum!

'I say you fellows . . .'

In this painting Pandora is seen as a child/woman who opens the toy-box merely through curiousity. She is unaware of the likely consequences and does not see the evil and destructive potential of what she has found. It is the boys who are excided by the discovery of new playthings.

If there is a message to be communicated by the painting it is that apathy, self-centredness, naivety and lack of political awareness that are the necessary concomitants of greater evils like cruelty, greed and arrogance. We all share responsibility for the evils and miseries of the world.

Democratically processed.

This painting protests against the callous indifferences in which peoples are held by their military and political overlords. Civilian populations are perceived as mere pawns in their masters' nightmarish war games. This lack of humanity is equally lacking in regimes both capitalist or communist. The needs and greeds of armament manufacturers, international money systems and multinational companies disregard geographical and political boundaries.

There is also an obscene assumption by British and American leaders that British and American lives are more important than the lives of people in other countries especially if they are third world countries. People are treated as a commodity in international trade-offs – and usually as a commodity of little worth. Although this attitude of politicians is most blatant and overt towards people of Third World countries there is little doubt that in a critical situation the populations of Europe and America would receive the same scant regard for their welfare, safety and human dignity.

'Democratically Processed'
Oil on canvas

Alison Allnutt

Christine Voge

I'm not a great debater or even a conversationalist – when it comes to expressing my feelings and thoughts about the world, I would much rather distil them through the medium of my work.

I see my photography as a document of other people's experiences, but also a document of how I feel about them, and how I relate my own past experiences to theirs. Photography has become an extension of my whole being – it looks complicated in the print and yet it's so simple . . . it's like learning to eat: first we fumble awkwardly with the spoon, and then we become experts.

When I was asked to submit work for 'Pandora's Box', I asked myself what the full import of participating in the show was to me. I am sure that many, if not most women today, must feel the way I do about the state of the world. It seems to me that so much evil has been unleashed on the world in recent years that indeed one can only hope for a series of miracles to restore it to a semblance of sanity. Sometimes I wake in the morning so paralysed with disillusionment that there seems no point in making it through the day but I just cling to life because of a hope that one day we will witness the triumph of truth. **Women, have for centuries been the scapegoats for all that is wrong with the world, and we have on the whole unquestioningly embraced the role allotted to us by the other half of humanity. I think a lot of women feel displaced from their rightful position on earth: desperately seeking our heritage, we find we have very little. We are deprived of a sense of history – our history is fragmented and, on the whole, recorded through the eyes and minds of men. Few women to date have been credited with anything of positive or lasting value. And this makes them/us/me angry.** How can that anger, that sense of being deeply wronged, ever be purged, cleansed from us in a matter of months or years, when we have centuries,

Untitled photograph

millennia, of unwittingly being consigned to the slagheap of life while our male counterparts have run off with the spoils? There are those, I know, for whom our recent awakening is but a bad dream soon to be erased by the drifting sands of time. But once awakened, how can we submit voluntarily to yet another injection of morphine? We need to find the means to make our awareness understood and assimilated – before it's too late.

My first pictures had little in common with my present range of subjects as I had not yet begun to use the camera as a channel for my deeper feelings. In fact, even after purchasing my first camera, I was afraid of threatening my husband's security by taking pictures, which sounds ridiculous now. I owe a lot of my technical knowledge to my present husband, a Danish photojournalist, but as far as professional confidence is concerned, it really took my first group exhibition to give me a firm belief in my ability. That was when I looked at my pictures on the wall alongside everyone else's and said to myself: you *do* know what

you're doing. I felt a great sense of direction then which has occasionally deserted me since – but, thank God, it always returns to me.

Often, when I take pictures, I feel oddly distant from the subject, as well as involved. It's an odd combination. I can't let any initial self-confidence of the people I'm photographing at the time affect me, otherwise I will fail to capture them. What always amazes me, is how many things can appear in a photograph I was only marginally aware of at the time of taking it; sometimes the glint of an eye, or a gesture that I fail to take note of at the time. I don't like setting up a picture – I might make a few little adjustments, like remove something that's in the way of the camera, but normally I like to get people as they are, in their environment. It's hard to avoid a contrived picture, because many people will behave differently as soon as they know a photographer is present. The big secret is to make such a nuissance of myself that they start to ignore me out of total boredom and exhaustion. In fact, the less

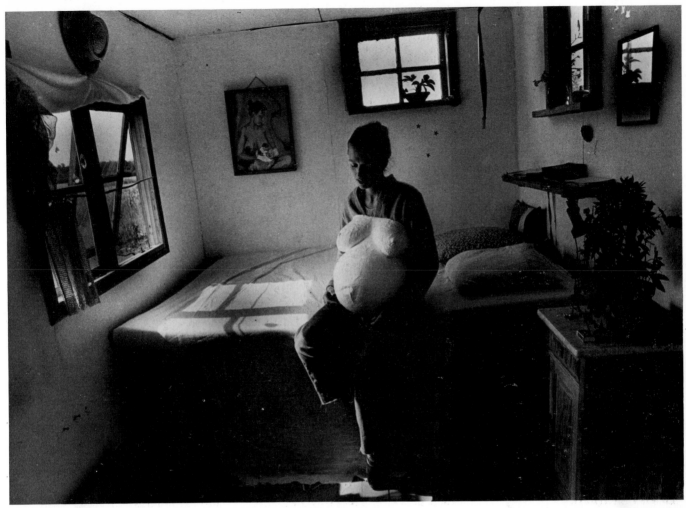

Untitled photograph

seriously people take me, the more likely I am to get 'the' picture! I think 75% of it really comes from entering the spirits of people, places, things: I can *be*, actually *be* all the elements of my picture for that fleeting moment it takes to click the shutter. Sometimes I thinkthat the camera is magic – I understand how the Indians were frightened that their souls would be captured in the camera if they allowed their photograph to be taken. **With the present exhibition, I didn't gear my choice of pictures to any selection panel, imagined or real, but submitted what I felt to be my best and most significant work. There was a set of photographs taken in a strip club in my home town of Indianapolis, as well as a scene in a Yugoslav mosque. Both aim to expose the awkward and unhappy relationship between the sexes as I perceive it.** In the mosque, a solitary woman prays in the obscurity of the upper platform, while hordes of men congregated in the main area below. I could barely see the woman in the darkness, and was shocked at first to have seen her at all because I wasn't even sure she had the right to be there.

There is no reliable way to predict the public's reaction to any given picture, nor can you ever achieve control of the viewer's interpretation of your work. The world is made up of such a medley of sensibilities and personal experiences that no matter how you strive to eradicate misunderstanding, it always reappears. I don't spend a lot of time analysing what makes me gravitate towards a certain theme – so often the moment is fleeting, and you just have to grab it.

Christine Voge

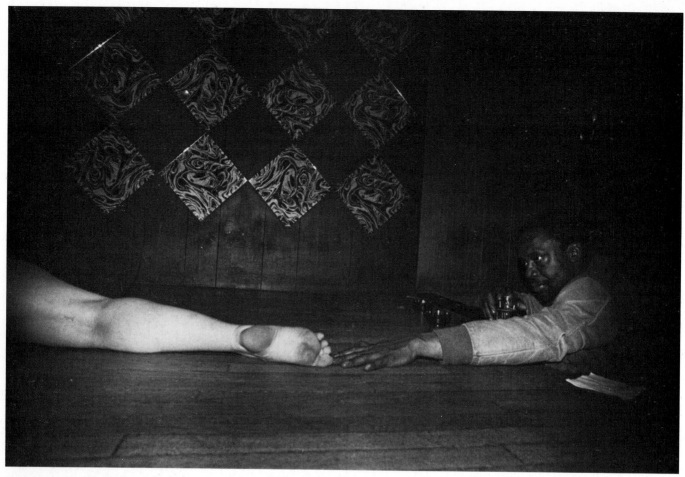

Indianapolis Strip Club, 1982
Photograph

The stripclub was in the heart of Indianapolis, right across from the Greyhound bus station. I was very fortunate to be allowed to take the pictures, because it's not everyday that you can walk right in to such a club and make yourself at home. The women in there were all for sale or rent – none of your look don't touch routine – and the club was owned and run by a woman, too. The strippers were self-conscious and made me feel unwelcome. When they challenged me, I told them I was taking the pictures for myself, which was absolutely true at the time. I started talking to them and just warmed to them. Listening is the important thing, really. I didn't reveal too much about myself, although they asked me a lot of questions. The club was most definitely mixed: there were black and white customers, strippers and prostitutes. Amongst them all there was this one black man who seemed displaced, solitary, alienated from his own race. He spent most of the evening drunk, hurling insulting comments at the women on the quality of their respective performances. In some strange way he wasn't lustful . . . it was as though he were playing the part of a man he didn't truly feel himself to be . . . a sort of caricature. I felt he was a man who was always disappointed, looking for some pie-in-the-sky dream of the typical male. He was lying back and saying 'make me feel good' . . . and feeling they should do more for him than they did. There wasn't really anything or anyone who could revive him. At that moment when he touched the stripper's leg, he seemed serious: it was the only time he seemed serious throughout the whole evening. And I managed to catch that.

Christine Voge

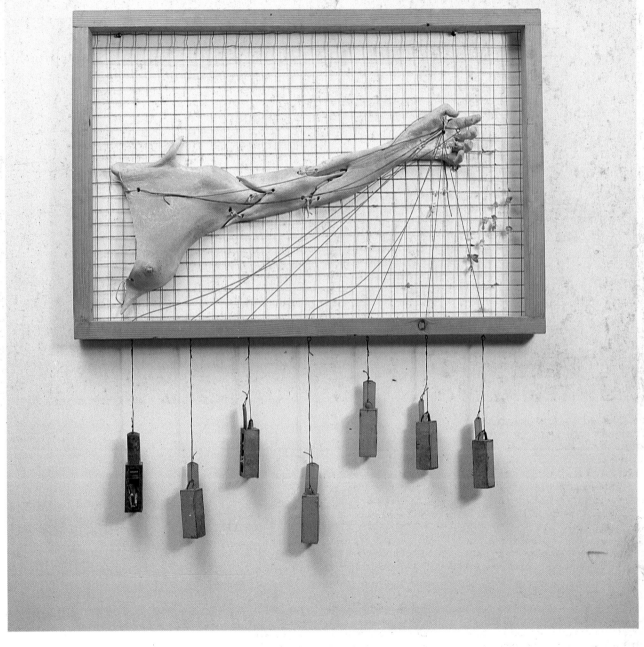

June Raby
Tension, 1982
Clay, wood and metal, 24 x 36 ins.

Catherine McWilliams
Irish Landscape II
Acrylic collage on paper, 22 x 30 ins.

Elena Samperi
Inside the Box
Mixed media

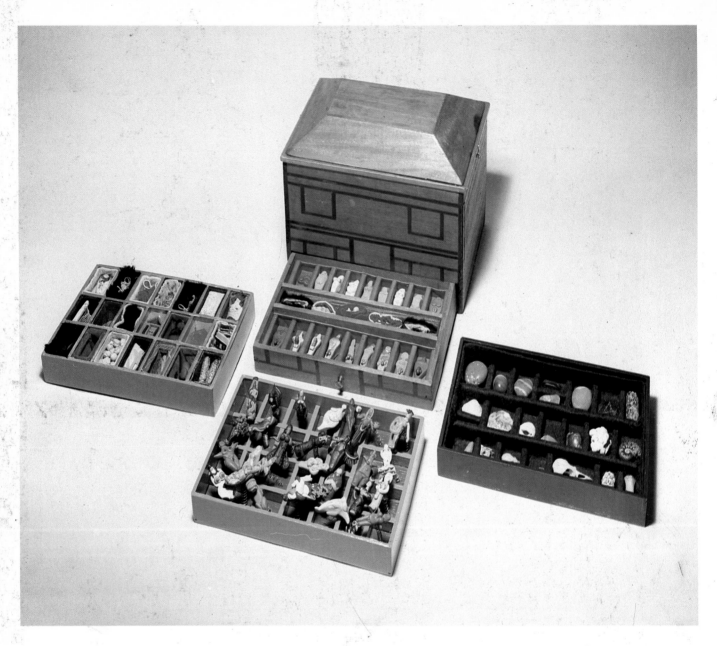

Louise Baker
Pandora's Box
Mixed media

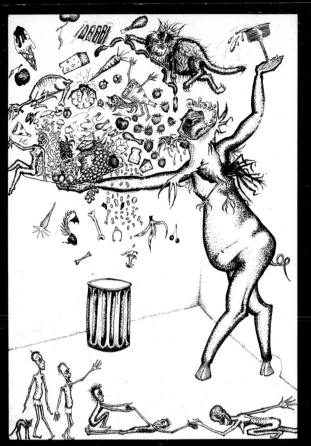

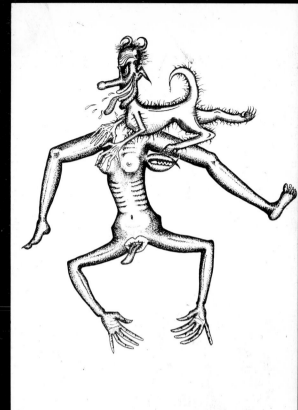

Gluttony
Ink drawing
11.5 x 8 ins.

Lust
Ink drawing
11.5 x 8 ins.

Avarice
Ink drawing
11.5 x 8 ins.

Envy
Ink drawing
11.5 x 8 ins.

Tessa Pollitt

I have never done an honest day's work in my life.

I left school in 1976 and began my education.

In 1977 I joined The Slits with Ari, Viv and Paloma. Our music was of primary importance to be able to express our passion into other people's lives.

Music moves people and as women we tried to take our music as far as possible, both physically and emotionally, internationally.

Dealing with high-powered companies, contracts, bullshit had nothing to do with our vision of what could be.

We began to concentrate our strengths individually. Whilst I was in The Slits we were always travelling and immediately after I left I headed for East Africa, where I spent two months travelling around between Sudan and Ethiopia.

My drawings have always been, in some way, a strong reflection of my feelings. Whilst I was playing they tended to be smaller and more intro-spective, intense and often filled with self-loathing. Since the end of The Slits I have been able to concentrate my outer influences into my work and find a more positive balance between what I feel inside and what I see outside.

This project gave me an oppor-tunity to involve my feelings towards rhythm, music and personal mythology, set against the darker aspects of my own character and the nature and relationship between the full spectrum of human attitudes. Black-White/Good-Evil. To reflect the bad in things is to become those things in oneself, but it is necessary as all these aspects exist within us, set against their opposites. By knowing these weaknesses in ourselves, by understanding them through our work, we can perhaps begin, at source, to eradicate them.

Any kind of creative act, whether it be music, writing, film, art, etc. should come from the deepest tunnels of feelings from our inner being (whether the inspirational flow comes from within projecting outwardly, or external observations and experiences entering within).

To have any kind of impact or effect upon those we wish to communicate with, it is of vital importance; to feel so intensely about something that it has to be explored and then released, like a baby waiting for its birth into the outside world, in the natural progres-sion of feeling and communicating.

The act of creating itself, in whatever form it may take, has an almost cleansing affect, in that it releases a certain amount of tension and satisfies a common desire to communicate with our fellow beings. Whether it is judged to be good or bad is not important. With the threat of so much destruction in the world today, that same energy could be channelled into its opposite – to create instead of destroy.

I have always found drawing a release for all kinds of polluting emotions: anger, frustration, sadness, also more brighter feelings of humour and joy, even in the simplest form of doodling. This is probably how I started to find myself during adolescence, through both music and drawing, a journey that continues on according to my life. I've used drawing as an imaginery person to talk to, a blank piece of paper being my chosen confidante, when words escape me and become a tangled mass of confusion and inadequacy inside my head. Some-times I might start out with a clear idea of where the picture is heading, but the finished result turns out to be quite different from that which I originally intended, almost uncannily, as if the paper or pen is disagreeing with me and suggesting an alternative idea.

This may occur because I allow the mistakes I make to change the direction of the picture, rather than erase them and start again, as if they were meant to happen.

In the same way I apply this to the way I live, if something appears to go wrong, it must have happened for a reason, so there is no reason to get downhearted, simply change course due to the diversion.

Our eyes are like a camera projecting images onto the screen of our minds. We cannot censor what we see, unless we blindfold ourselves, only what we choose to mirror back to the world, according to the impact it has on us. Whatever affects us most will leave an imprint on our minds, where it will be churned over, according to past experiences and individual opinion, and then reflected back into our chosen medium.

It is therefore important to keep an open mind and try to experience as much as possible, not only things that give us pleasure, but to feed our minds with as wide a range of feelings and images as we can, in order to refer and reflect them in our communication to others, and also to feed the imagination, which will be in accordance with our culture, condi-tioning and individual experiences.

In the drawings I have done for this exhibition, I have tried not to put too much emphasis on time, place or particular objects, to show that the prevailing evils amongst us have existed in all time and all places. Certain images like a dustbin, oil syphon or ladder merely represent images of things in my lifetime to explain a certain point, it is not what they are that is important but what they represent.

The reason for continual use of half-animal, half-human is to show the more bestial side of our nature, the less feeling and more instinctive side; not necessarily a bad thing. It is we humans who have corrupted the names of harmless animals, human-ising them with such labels as – 'fat as a pig', 'you dirty dog'.

Our instinctive natural selves are fading away as we become more aware of the growing power of our minds.

I have always had a fascination for the macabre and the ridiculous aspects of life, which is why perhaps I enjoy the works of Wilhelm Busch and the stories and drawings of Strewelpeter. Both quite absurd and with a lot of black humour. For a child, quite menacing images to suffocate the threatening night with.

The importance to me of this show being all women's work is due only to the fact that at present, and in the past, men have continued to have a stranglehold in the art world, that is in terms of business and actual painters; galleries and critics are predominantly male. At this point, therefore, the strength of the collective experience of women artists working together is positive and inspirational, though ultimately art is genderless. Because the sexes are so different, perhaps at this stage there is a finer female aesthetic still unspoilt, which will remain so as long as women continue to value their own qualities rather than compete or mimic their aggressive male contenders. There is much which can and should be explored but not exploited by women artists individually. Art itself can never be a collective experience, it is essentially subjective, a personal experience. What is truly important is not the sex or race of the artist but the essential human qualities that are involved in producing the work, only the most powerful and sincere of which should be reflected in one's work.

The only way to learn is the hard way, for that way one can really learn, like the child fascinated by fire, until it finds out the fire burns. The instinctive curiosity of Pandora ('the rich in gifts', 'the all giving') did not kill her or the human race but laid the foundation for us to learn and make a choice to continue the struggle for good against evil.

Without following our curiosity and thirst for knowledge we would remain in darkness, forever ignorant.

I chose the Seven Deadly Sins: Gluttony, Lust, Avarice, Envy, Pride, Wrath and Sloth; to represent the evils of mankind, and suggest that the box or vase contained the emotions of humans, which, unless we learn how to channel and understand, could and have been the downfall of the human race.

We must constantly be aware of the power of our emotions so that we can learn to rule them and not allow them to rule us, or we will find ourselves in a frustrating state of confusion.

Pride
Ink drawing
8 x 11.5 ins.

Sloth
Ink drawing
8 x 11.5 ins.

Wrath
Ink drawing
8 x 11.5 ins.

If we become a victim of our emotions we are lost, for we become too involved in ourselves in an introspective way, losing sight of our purpose and chaining ourselves to material and physical desires instead of aiming outwardly for a higher selfless state of being.

Alternatively, we could learn to master and confront our emotions until we have rooted out the badness that breeds a cancer of mistrust, prejudice and hate.

The most important aspect of the exhibition, the myth and life itself, is the remaining positive hope in its fleeting but abundant embrace.

Tessa Pollitt

Katya Coupland

Katya Coupland

My work is generally concerned with objects and interiors. The objects containing references so personal that they become universal. Often the references are unconscious ones, the reasons why I chose them becoming clear only in time or when I find myself repeating a theme. Sometimes the objects act as symbols, though not consciously chosen as such, interpretable in a number of ways perhaps.

My work is concerned with narrative though it took me a long time to accept it, because I think my interest lay in a less literal meaning of the word. Perhaps a narrative could form itself out of a given set of circumstances. Perhaps the objects became clues to a personally invented story on the part of each viewer.

The images I use are always recognisable. I have never felt tempted to dispense with representational imagery and use purely abstract form. There are passages of purely abstract use of paint within a painting though. The eclectic use of style, imagery and handling of paint in my work is reflective of the age. Being bombarded on all sides by a visual imagery, contemporary and also drawn from the past, my reaction is magpie-like.

The subject matter I use is never by it's nature fantastic, not mythical or religious, always relatively common objects. The exploding handbag idea is one which I had begun to work on about a year prior to deciding to contribute to this theme exhibition. The image of the exploding handbag seemed like a natural metaphor for Pandora's Box. Though as I have already said the images I choose are rarely consciously chosen metaphors. **The connection I see between the image of the exploding handbag and the myth of Pandora's Box is partly to do with woman's acceptance of responsibility for looking after the fundamental physical and mental health of humanity, with the running of day to day living. We learn at an early age that the elements needed to survive in the society outside are contained in the bag the mother carries. It's expected that the**

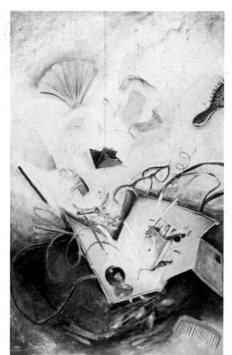

Exploding Handbag
Oil on canvas

mother should bear the overall responsibility for the welfare of the family and that she should be blamed should the next generation suffer from her neglect. In my work in this show none of the individual objects bursting from the bag have any specific symbolic meaning. They are objects familiar to me and with personal connections.

The artists to whom I looked initially were men. When my first interest in painting crystalised, at school I wasn't aware of any women artists on whom I could model myself. The notable artists, it seemed were all men though that fact didn't seem particularly relevant at the time. My Art School training (Fine Art, Middlesex Polytechnic) was inevitably dominated by male tutors though I think that there was an awareness of the imbalance in the situation. However there were tutors who contributed to my confidence by taking me seriously despite the unfashionable nature of my work at that point in time.

Happily things are changing and as more women are becoming committed artists a different perspective is emerging which is perhaps the result of a less monocular vision. Even in the sixties the Art that I considered contemporary, and felt reflective of the age I lived in, was dominated by male artists. Now I find myself surrounded by artists that are women and in an altogether more supportive atmosphere.

I would not in any way consider myself a political person and my art does not spring from any desire to instruct or inform. Though the myth of Pandora's Box is hard to see in any other than a political light in the context of a women's show, I suppose I would like to think that at best my pictures might provide material for the viewer to use as a mirror, though this is an afterthought and not why the pictures are made. Even though I have no clear political intentions behind my work it wouldn't be true to say that there are never any political references contained within a painting. They are there along with all the other intellectual, emotional, spiritual and historical references that go to make up a work.

I have no axe to grind about my situation as a woman artist, though I realise that this is due to the efforts of a number of women, who changed the whole climate of acceptance of artists who happen also to be women, during the past decade.

The difficulties I have experienced in functioning as an artist have to a large extent been due to my family responsibilities, choosing to have a child and looking after elderly relations. However though these are clearly problems relating to the fact that I am a woman in this society I could not say that I would not have had equal but different problems as a male artist or even as a single person without family commitments.

Art, it seems, often with its rather intangible rewards, cannot hope to be of interest, by and large to a society which is programmed to be consumers of a light diet of easily digested products. That is the situation with which artists have to come to terms

The First Exploding Handbag
Oil on canvas 48 x 36 ins.

regardless of their sex. Until the work of artists is not only glimpsed in galleries for a matter of moments but actually in people's homes and work places, the real value of a piece can't hope to be considered or appreciated.

More women than men buy my work. Whether its because the ideas behind my work are easier to relate to for women, or they have less prejudices against women than men do, is hard to say.

I live in North London with my husband and daughter. I earn my living by teaching Painting and Drawing in Islington Adult Education Institute and painting backgrounds and making models for stills photography in the advertising industry. I have a studio in Wapping which I manage to get into on average two days a week at present. In addition to which I am able to spend one day etching.

Katya Coupland

. . . But he feeds on us, like all of them. His whole life, his art is protected by women. Which of us could say that?
Which of us, Clara, hasn't had to take that leap
out beyond our being women
to save our work? or is it to save ourselves?

(from Paula Becker to Clara Westhoff by Adrienne Rich.)

Part I. At fourteen my future appeared to me in frozen stills, sepia tinted daydreams. In one I sit before an oval dressing table, ruched frills to the floor, gazing into its hinged mirrors. On its polished glass surface rests an ivory-backed brush set and a huge powder puff. My adult self, in a 1950's strapless ball gown, head tilted sightly to the right brushes the iced ripples of her elegant coiffure. She is reflected indistinctly in the mirror along with an enticing double bed and the handsome figure of a husband wearing a suit and tie.

In the other I stand laughing in a loose circle of friends, face clear and hair tumbling over my shoulders. I have on a large brown coat and a striped scarf, poised to return to paint in my London studio.

In retrospect, although naïve, the choice seems remarkably perceptive and more than a question of lifestyle. The hours I spent painting in my room in a Buenos Aires suburb felt like taking swims in a different kind of water that made me feel more alive. Instead of curling my eyelashes and despite failing art 'O' level twice, I set out to make paintings.

It was ten years before I could work without looking over my shoulder. A son, lovers and what I can only describe as an unrecognised desire to be the subject of a great painting drove me to turn my back on it for about four years. I returned like a lost and homesick traveller to liberated lands, camped out in the biggest room in the house and learnt to work with fragmented images, using scrap materials which reflected how I lived rather than some romantic notion. I

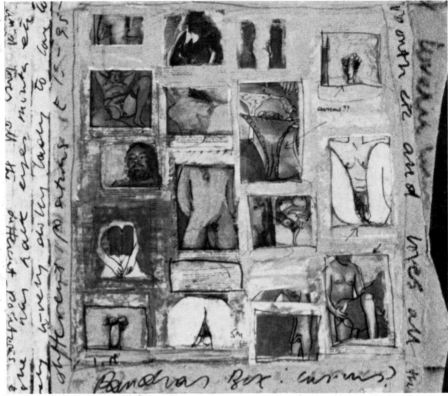

Details of "Man Made"

no longer waited for time, money or permission.

Part II **It is not incidental to how I breathe, paint, talk, earn money or anything else that I am a woman who has become a mother, a feminist, a revolutionary socialist but neither is the way I do these things prescribed by my politics. Art is not above gender or class and can serve reactionary or progressive ends but it is also specific to itself and not a substitute for other forms of action.** There are more effective ways of sharing a vision than spending months painting an image to hang in a gallery patronised by obnoxious Tory connoisseurs who would buy canvases stained with the blood of peasant women if the proportions were right. The thought of succeeding on their terms makes me want to start lying, behaving myself, smiling too

much, combing my hair and throwing up.

The crucial factor in the relationship between art and politics lies in what sector of society appropriates it, with or without the artist's consent. Frida Kahlo and Diego Rivera worked figuratively in revolutionary Mexico but at the time of the Russian revolution traditional painters admired by Lenin were Tsarists, while the avante-garde supported the Bolsheviks and formed a movement which expanded into popular culture unparalleled vigour. The mandarins of the New York art establishment condemned abstract work as a Communist plot until Stalin denounced it as bourgeois and institutionalized social realism as the 'art of the people', upon which abstract painters became the epitomy of the capitalist dream. Pieces by members of the Proletkult now change hands at exhorbitant prices on the

East Side.

The social context, politics and gender of the artist, the composition of the audience and the content of the work, are all variables in a complex picture. A constant factor has been a deliberate blindness to the work of women and a patriarchal bias in the images produced of us, the old fascist favourites, the mother and the whore overshadowing the silent prescence of daughters, sisters and wives. Despite the problems of defining a women's, let alone a feminist art, we all carry our common history into the studio on our backs and I think this gives a curiously intimate quality to the work; the sense of an old friend who can still surprise you.

Part III When I came back to painting in 1975 I worked very badly every day but it was a question of survival and I didn't care. I dived into my own space to make huge sails dipped in coloured wax, cloth etchings stitched together and dreaming map drawings. I worked on a collective project with two other women (Kassandra Pardee and Sarah Ainslie) and used all the information at my disposal.

I was a shop steward, looked after my son and stayed up all night scribbling, tacking, staining, sweeping dust and old bus tickets into little bags. Figurative work seemed very restrictive to me and I was inspired by other women, listened to music and sometimes fell in love with inappropriate men. I won a Southern Arts bursary and had a joint exhibition at the Arnolfini both of which deeply depressed me. Unhappy, I painted heavy bitumen black spirals. When I felt better I made drawings of skies and kites and hung rows of broken glass and strips of cloth to cast shadows over them.

In the spring of 1982 I read Monique Wittig's dazzling *Les Guerrilliers* and painted some impressions of it. That painting although only half successful, pulled me into increasingly more figurative work and I painted a bloody version of Gentileschi's *Judith* and multi-coloured images of Bolivia after a journey there. I had already developed a way of making working

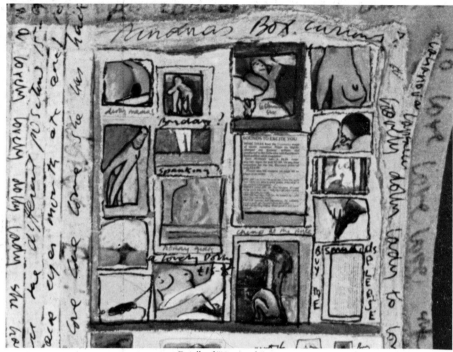

Details of "Man-made"

surfaces by nailing an old blanket to the wall, covering it with hemmed cotton scraps from jumble sales, cutting around three of the sewn edges and sticking the flap to the blanket with paste or emulsion before priming the whole area. I draw on these stiff skins and use oils and also powdered stage pigments mixed with a gel medium. Sometimes paintings work straight away but a piece may give me trouble and make me jump up and down and attack it with different ideas and materials. If the attack goes too far I destroy it altogether and put it in the bin but interesting things can happen in this way. I am now working on a large piece about life models.

Part IV I worked on the 'Pandora' paintings for about four months and it was a fine time of waking up to breathe and paint what I had dreamed about the night before.

Under the Breast the Bone was painted from photographs of women who have inspired me, friends and strangers, my Pandoras. This painting challenged the negative assumptions of the male myth and substituted a rib cage, a pelvis and individual faces for the bruised tits and bums of the first.

For *Dressed in Glittering Raiment, They Drank Heavily Laughing Loudly* I asked three friends to spend an evening together dressed for each other's pleasure in the sort of clothes women generally wear for men while I recorded the event with slides and photographs. I had originally intended to poke fun at the myth but a more complicated picture emerged. What happened is in the painting along with some of what I was thinking about at the time.

Part V Writing all this has been like pulling out a bad tooth and then then having to wear it around my neck. I can't possibly write any more.

Penny Woolcock

Peggie Radford

The imagery of my work is generated by the medium. Foam rubber, nylon and ceramics. The imagery is developed from my enjoyment of circuses, fairground art, seaside postcards and the satisfaction of art which is obvious and amusing.

I particularly like the work of Rousseau, Stanley Spencer and Peter Blake, all of whom inspire my sculpture in different ways. I have been compared with Beryl Cook and, although there are similarities, I do not draw on life around me or people I know for inspiration. I try to portray the ideal extrovert woman who enjoys being flamboyant and theatrical and is, like myself, on the threshold of middle age. Perhaps they are me as I would like to be?

I have been astonished by the strong reactions they evoke in people. Many enjoy their blatant brazenness and think them extremely funny – children always find them hilarious – and some are disgusted. In fact a larger proportion of this latter category are men. As long as they cause some strong emotion in people, I do not mind. I see no reason why art should be belittled because it is humorous. My work is constantly being attacked as being degrading to women. I find the image of a woman as a stylized sex object very funny. I can watch 'Miss World' or open 'Page Three' with no hint of outrage, so if my sculpture is offensive to some people, I am afraid I am not in a position to judge the validity of such comment.

I trained as a fashion designer, taught art at various secondary schools and have for the past ten years been bringing up a family. The demands of which, although giving little time to my work, are to an extent mitigated by working in a secure environment where financial constraints do not force me to only produce work which I know will sell. However, there are times when the frustration of having to stop midway through a piece of work to attend to a domestic matter is very trying. I work for my own self-satisfaction. I am delighted when my work is patronised but whether it is loathed or loved I do not experience any pressure to satisfy the expectations of anyone else.

Pandora's Box produced a host of emotions in me. It would contain the ultimate horror which for me is war. Plague, pestilence, famine, hallucination and madness are out of the control of mankind but war can be controlled if the will exists. There is in man, but I suggest not in woman, a primeval death wish which is excited by the temptation of opening the box.

The temptation is all the more difficult to resist if the box has no external warning signs. Even more so if it is held by a woman. Woman who is the embodiment of fertility and continuing life holding a box which contains death. Women have in history and legend been tempted – Eve by the Serpent being the first. But they in their own turn have tempted men as Eve did Adam.

The image of the soldier in a gas or radiation mask, de-humanised and unrecognisable, evokes in me a chill feeling that if the mask were removed there would not be a face underneath but a blank machine.

I wanted the contrast of the bright, humorous imagery and the horror of the contents of the box and the contrast of the soft human form and the hard ceramic soldiers' heads.

I have not exhibited my work much, partly as I have felt that only recently have I achieved a good technical standard and organising my time to work, let alone make contacts, has been difficult. I was involved however in a women's exhibition last year. A group of local women artists came together because we all felt we wanted to show our work and were bound by a common aim. Many had children and fitted their art into the spare moments of the day and worked in spite of external pressures. We received a lot of local coverage and I personally received publicity. In many ways people jumped to the conclusion that an all-women show must be feminist and as my work was considered sexist I received some criticism. Somehow an all-male exhibition never causes comment.

I fear that some may see the 'Pandora's Box' exhibition as a group of women declaring their independence because they feel they cannot compete with men. I do hope this is not so. So much can be gained by both the artists and the public. The interpretation of the theme, the techniques used are all the more interesting when viewed through the eyes of one sex only.

My work has evolved through experimentation, first with ceramic sculpture which led to a mixture of ceramics and fabrics and became predominantly 'soft' sculpture in 1980. I was inspired by a visit to the USA and since returning have evolved my own technique through trial and error. I have not met others working in a similar medium locally so I am only learning by my own mistakes. **My sculptures are not sexist because I only make women. However I find the medium lends itself to their soft fleshy appearance. I like to think they give tactile satisfaction as well as visual. I intend to make more men in the future but I see them as being only in supportive roles.**

As I work from a studio in my home, I am restricted to the size of the sculpture. I would eventually like to produce work on a larger scale but I find at present life-size figures are the biggest size permits.

I hope I have reached a time in my life when I can reflect and put to good use my experience and to start to fulfill any capabilities I might have. I am just beginning to achieve an artistic style which is special to me and will, I hope, continue to develop.

Peggy Radford
The Ice Cream Lady
Mixed media, 52 ins. high

Dierdre Shulman
Jessica, 1983
Pastel on paper, 27 x 20 ins.

Gill Calvert
Women's Estate
Oil on canvas

Myths and legends are sometimes based on truths, sometimes on fears, and sometimes on superstitions. The quality of a great myth is its power to transcend its own time and provide relevance or meaning to any society.

The particular version of the Pandora myth that I was familiar with and have always been fascinated by, is the story where Pandora's crime is curiosity, and her punishment the release of evils and plagues onto the world. The horrific conclusion of the story, however, is alleviated by the presence of Hope, who Pandora discovers and releases when all the other spirits have flown. But even as a child I found the story's end filled me with a curious tension rather than the relief that I think was intended. I hated the idea that the others had a head start, when Pandora hurriedly slammed the lid on Hope, and felt despair that there weren't more Hopes, especially as hope seems so much less concrete than misery, plague or sorrow.

The fact that the Pandora legend exists at all could be seen as reason enough for holding an all-women's exhibition. There is no doubt that all the Pandora myths are criticising women to a lesser or greater degree. She is the classical equivalent to Eve, her curiosity/desire to know leads her to open the box/bite the apple, thus inflicting evil upon men. Although the stories were written a long time ago, in far more prejudiced and superstitious days, they anger women today, because they are unjust, and because they represent an attitude against women that has still to be dispelled.

So what actually is the relevance of the story to us, and how loosely or broadly can it be interpreted? Suppose a woman had written the tale, what would it mean then? If I take the story out of its patriarchal context, I find myself returning to my childhood response.

I identify with Pandora. I too would have been unable to contain myself from opening the tantalising box. Like Pandora, I
would also have to know, to discover – whatever the cost. And is that necessarily evil? Is not 'to know', 'to understand'?

My pictures are an attempt to understand my immediate world. I happen to have been born a woman and to be living in the 1980s, so these things *have* to inform my art – but they are simply reflected in my pictures, they are never the reason a picture is painted. Whether my subject is a playground, a group of skinheads, a pregnant woman or a shopping centre, the picture is a response, and never a tract or dogmatic statement. I like to draw people, and they are always the subject of my pictures. Although fashions, ideas, styles, environment, politics, technology and language evolve and change the surface of our world, human beings do not change – that is why myths retain their significance. It is simply the circumstances or the setting of the story that have to change.

Pandora is me, or any woman, examining the possibilities today, seeing the pitfalls (evils and plagues) that exist, and have always existed in one form or another. Any of us can take the decision to open the box: i.e. 'to discover', and we all have the freedom to decide how best to tackle these discoveries.

Jessica is an eighteen-year-old girl I know, who has kissed her dolls good-night every evening since she was five. She is engaged, and wants to marry Derek next year. Her visions of marriage and motherhood are neat, pretty and unrealistic. Her games of mummies and daddies and her romanticism are fed by the literature she reads. She is a talented young actress, who has been urged by teachers to apply for drama school, but she is working in Tesco's because she wants to save up, and because Derek didn't want her to go away. It is quite a dark picture at the moment, despite the brightness of her smile, and the colours of the confetti, but Jessica is making choices all the time. She chose not to apply to drama college, although the encouragement
and opportunities presented themselves. She chose Derek, although other boys in her year would have been very keen for her to go off to study. Men are not to blame for Jessica's story. **As in the Pandora story we can see the concrete evils, the screaming babies, the despair and loneliness: but there is, underneath it all, that little squeak of hope preventing either story from ever ending, for there is the promise that beyond the gloom there may be light.**

Possibly Jessica will decide later that she has the confidence to go to college; that she doesn't need Derek, dolls and romantic fiction. Whether she does or not: whether she buries herself or fights loose is ultimately immaterial – the possibility; the hope exists, and that is enough.

Women everywhere are searching for ways of transcending their biological function, or compromising it with their creative potential. Having babies is creative, but very tiring – it is difficult to have babies and paint pictures: the two activities are not very compatible.

Until this century, therefore, women haven't really painted pictures because they weren't given the option on childbearing. Also, of course, as official childrearers they were not given the status to paint. Consequently the idea of 'women's art' is still relatively new. And the woman as artist has yet to find her voice. She lacks confidence because she has no heritage, only centuries of male images to emulate and learn from; and these may not be particularly relevant. Just as a soprano would not be expected to sing a tenor or barritone part, a woman artist should not need to adopt the timbre of male visual vocabulary. Until she finds her own register, a woman's voice might sound squeeky or strident, but I'm certain that in the end she will find her range and sing her subject eloquently.

June Raby

I have always loved drawing, painting and making things. It has continually been fulfilling and a tremendous source of pleasure and comfort to me, always there, unlike so many other things in my life which has been quite volatile.

In the last ten years, my work has increased in importance and gives me a certain drive, which however, is tempered by the need to bring up my daughter and earn money.

Through my experiences, I have learnt the need to communicate with people and nearly always

Detail of "Tension"

work along these lines, discussing through my work problems that I see or feel in my own life or on wider themes.

Art, whether sculpture, writing or acting is a way of communicating with others and hopefully saying something of value which can be open to discussion. Lately my work has been concerned with manipulation, for example, people climbing over others to achieve success and the government's media manipulation of the Falklands affair. It is often figurative, concerned with self-discovery and understanding the world in which we live.

There is little doubt of the discrimination experienced by women trying to take part in a hitherto male dominated area. Recently several important art shows have not included women and very few people in the media have shown surprise or disgust. As soon as an alternative womans show is organised, it is somehow wrong, using the argument that we should not parry their selfish contempt by emulating them.

Women do not yet have the strong power network of males and a womans show, demonstrating by its title the need for it, is an excellent way of getting women together, not competing against each other for the favours of men in power. Those women who do run galleries and those men sympathetic to the argument are nevertheless intimidated by financial pressures not to concern themselves with feminist art or even exclusively female artists, in anything other than a token manner. Male art is not necessarily what the majority of people want, it is illogical that this art – if derived from male experience – will strike a chord in females in the same way as womens art. It is an argument that can be expressed in many ways, for example all sport is geared to what man can do better than women, despite our proven greater stamina.

Art colleges have a higher proportion of female students than most other establishments of higher education. This is partly, I believe, because women have a great desire to communicate and share their lives and experiences with others – they have not been taught to compete however, and the tutors in art colleges are predominantly male and the higher you look the more men there are. This reinforces the status quo, giving women little confidence to believe that they will be able to achieve anything in this male world of art, despite the high standard of much of their work.

This obviously leads one to ask what success and achievement really are, what are the competitors trying to prove and who to? To earn a living one must be paid and to do this one

must accept or be accepted by the establishment.

The economic weakness of women stresses the fact that men's work and achievements are taken more seriously than women's. Women's achievements, from child rearing to their creative work is denied importance. It is suggested that women are creative in bringing children into the world and therefore their creative urge is suppressed by their caring and supportive roles. I would suggest the reverse, their personal experiences promote awareness. Child rearing

despite being so immensely important is today not thought of as real work, or if it is people do it for love not money (and therefore are dependant), like nursing the sick or caring for the elderly – until you become a consultant or a surgeon!

The myth of Pandora's Box still has relevance today, just as in the past, many men have distrusted and blamed women for ills caused by themselves, so some still do today.

Women are the obvious physical creators of our future, they give birth, opening the box, are women the 'box'?

Male physical strength and aggression has always been a hold over women, while women have not even been in control of their fertility. These obvious differences have become tempered by the fact that fewer jobs require brute strength and fewer women are involuntarily pregnant. We still need to change attitudes which have evolved over thousands of years based on the former premise.

'Our country' she will say, 'Throughout history has treated me as a slave . . . in fact as a woman I have no country.'' Virginia Woolf: *Three Guineas*.

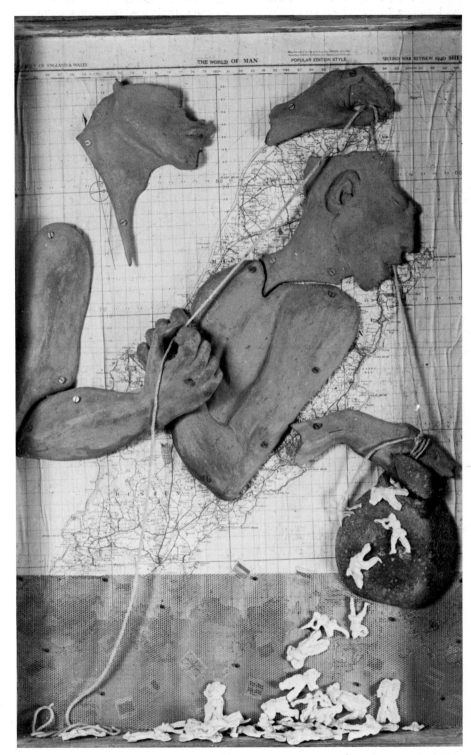

Pandora's Box
Clay, wood and string, 35 x 24 x 4 ins.

June Raby

Elana Samperi

Elana Samperi

Deep in the sacred caves of the mountain Tarcarcuna, overlooking the deep waters of the gulf of Darien, the spirit of the Goddess Mu, giant Blue Butterfly Lady, still lingers lovingly, protecting the women of the Cuna tribe.

In the days before the world began, Mu gave birth to the sun and taking Her sun as Her lover, She gave birth to the moon. Mating with her grandson Moon, She brought forth the stars, so many that they filled the heavens. Then mating with the stars, the sacred womb of Mu once again stirred with life so that in this way she brought forth all the animals and plants. It is for this reason that Cuna people remember that Mu gave birth to the universe – created all that exists . . . .

Close to the caves of Tarcarcuna, stands the sacred grove of saptur, trees whose fruit contain the juice of the menstrual blood of Mu. On the ground the young one lies being as one with the earth, as the older women toss the sacred soil upon her. Gathering in a circle about her, they sit on the benches to form the Ring of Protection, smoke rising from their pipes as incense, invoking the spirit of Mu. Then removing the covering of earth, the women take the young one and paint the red juice of the saptur, the menstrual blood of Mu, upon her face – chanting their blessing on her life, honouring her with the dance of the new womanhood . . . .

These are extracts from another myth, with the soothing effect of revaluing women and feminine principles. The Cuna people of Panama, like other non-european populations, seem to have escaped the temptation of making women the guilt-object of all evil on earth. Thinking about Pandora's myth I felt a strong desire to have a time machine in order to go back and seeing how it all began, how somebody first conceived the idea of throwing all the blame of what is evil onto only one part of the human race: women. In spite of my curiosity and the legitimate anxiety to know, I think that at this point of world history it would be very complicated, even for the most dedicated anthropologist,

A Beautiful Golem, 1983

philosopher, researcher, etc. to know, to find THE source (was there only one or, instead, different versions of the myth, manipulated according to 'historical' necessities?) Perhaps it would be easy to say that Pandora's myth was written by a male chauvinist, by a misogynist and that in fact Pandora was only an instrument used by the male God Jupiter who viciously tempted her . . . And to these ideas there could easily be an opposite answer, so it would go on forever in those usual male-female differences and superiority arguments . . .

In my work for this show I preferred to consider the effects of the myth on the life of women: once Pandora opened the box, consciously or unconsciously responsible, she placed herself in another box, a real box-prison whose influence has been tragically long-lasting . . . More than their male counterparts, women have suffered on this planet the effects of being incarcerated into box-houses, box-roles, box-suffocating torture chambers where their crucified

soul struggled like a captured butterfly in order to break free.

I asked myself many and many times what is the mechanism that allows oppression, the hinge establishing the roles of oppressor/oppressed. What is the responsibility of the victim towards its torturer? What is the responsibility of the oppressed populations of the earth towards their dictators. What is our responsibility as women in having allowed 'the other' to oppress us for so long?

Whoever put Pandora into a box, with or without her direct complicity, suffered, ultimately, the same pains of his 'victim'.

As Virginia Woolf says in *A Room of One's Own*: 'a liberated society can not exist if part of it is not free and liberated'. When women are free, all society will be free.

In this 1984, whose threatening sound is not only a literary reminiscence, we should all start to understand that the future of the human race depends on uniting and relating our responsibilities and not on separating them.

The oriental philosophies and ethics still so much in fashion have been telling us in every possible way to come out from the box compartments of our separate existences . . .

We should finally understand that male-female are not separated, antagonistic entities; the world balance, for too long lost, is strictly linked to the interrelation and equal capability of 'function-ing' of men and women. Women may choose the strategy of a separated struggle, it may be still necessary for some issues, but ultimate objectives should be to strive to unite all humans in the latest struggle of them all: our right to exist in a world free of terror and the right of our planet to continue to be in this universe . . .

I have always described my works as political, in the widest sense of the word, perhaps – I do not like boxes myself – but, yes, political either when I am using 'private' images or more 'public' ones.

In the works of this and other

shows, terror is painted on the faces of my female characters, not because I morbidly like to dwell on horror and fear but because I hope that through their direct recognition we can finally speed our way out of all this ... The horror inside my women, prison boxes, their dolls' houses, their mortal glass chambers is indeed joined to another element: these figures are oppressed but powerful and angry. The crucified butterfly was once a goddess Mu and inside the dolls' house the woman-child who was never allowed to grow has developed a third eye; they both shout in an outburst of rage, rage against the establishment perhaps but angry with themselves as well, trying to understand why and what is their share of responsibility in allowing the 'other' to keep them in boxes for so long ...

A Doll's House, 1982

Elana Samperi

Kathleen Michael

Kathleen Michael

Pandora lives in me. She is the all-giving mother who encourages me to open the mystery box of my life. As I live I create my own myth.

I believe that when a person is able to actualise their fantasies, to create their own reality they will live a personal myth. Most people take the life of another as an example and try to live in the same manner; never facing their own essence. They are born and they die within limits that are set by others.

I think the first word I learnt as a child was *why*. Curiosity is the motivating force of my life. I always want to understand what lies behind, beyond, or underneath.

There is always the chance that my curiosity will lead me and those associated with me into occasional chaos, but that is a risk I must take.

As in the myth of Pandora curiosity is normally viewed as a negative force. 'Curiosity killed the cat', is an old saying meant to instill fear in the adventuresome. I see fear as the antithesis of living life fully. 'There is nothing to fear but fear itself', is an adage my mother often quoted and my experience has proved it to be true. **When I become afraid to open the bottomless Pandoras box in myself my life is blocked and stagnant. Fortunately curiosity always comes to my rescue and pushes me to take the next chance that will bring the next change.**

Womanhood is symbolic of change. Within my body I possess a monthly cycle that is personal to me, and at the same time is connected to the cycles of the moon. Since women are born with this innate sense of change they are close to an essential quality of life.

As a woman I am aware of my potential for creativity. This feeling of creativity has not been represented in the form of a child, but in my own life. As the moon has its dark side so a creative life carries the side of destruction. When a new side of myself is beginning to unfold the old must be sacrificed.

The photographs express my myth as it has developed this far. I see myself

Untitled photograph

as half ancient and half modern woman. These two sides are always fighting for exposure and it is my task to allow them the release they need.

I was born in America, though I never felt comfortable with the culture.

My ancient side began to grow due to my association with my Middle Eastern relatives and my interest in old Egyptian societies. I can remember as a child sitting and looking at *The Book of Knowledge* on the subject of

Ancient Egypt and feeling a magic there that the present day world did not hold for me. I could not imagine living my entire life in America. I left San Francisco five years ago with a one-way ticket. I knew that the usual American two week tour of Europe would not satisfy me. I knew that for me to experience European life and its effect on me would take time.

I interpret my decision to come to Europe as a turning point as it was not until I took the step to leave America that I came alive with myself. I had to experience two marriages and my mother's death before I was free to follow my curiosity.

I was educated, as most people, that satisfaction in life comes from outside myself. I was given the programming that when a person finds unity with another to complete them all is bliss. I discovered this kind of thinking led to misconceptions in my relationships and the ultimate end of my marriages. The destruction of these marriages was the seed of creation for my inner unity.

The death of my mother was a shock that awoke me to the use of my own potential. My mother was a woman who died of unrequited love. She was a beautiful woman who did not enjoy her beauty for its own sake. Her experience as an American housewife in the 50's was a disappointment from which she never recovered. I remember saying to her before she died that her life had not been lived in vain. I took my mother's death as a symbol of my rebirth. I am now turning to reality the dreams dreamt by my mother and her mother before her.

'Dance for Na Na', was a command I heard in childhood and one I was glad to fulfill. I began to study ballet at the age of four and used to enjoy displaying my talents before my family. My grandmother took particular delight in these occasions. Whenever there was a program of ballet on television she would declare, 'there's my Kathy'. I, however, was more influenced by grandmothers singing in Arabic and the dancing I saw at family gatherings than ballet.

Untitled photograph

Kathleen Michael

I saw belly dancing performed for the first time in San Francisco and heard the voice of my ancient side speak to me again. I became fascinated with this dance form as it portrays in its movements the mystery and power of woman. And . . . I intend to create an atmosphere of magic for the audience when I dance, opening them to feelings of wonder and sensuality. I imagine myself to be a representation of a timeless woman touching places in the audience that have been lying dormant.

This ancient side is definitely the feminine within me and finds expression in dance. The modern side is expressed in the medium of photography. There is a further connection in that it was my mother who exposed me to dance and my father to photography.

Photography has proven to be a tool to enrich my powers of intuition and as a projection of experiences within. I decide to take a photo because the subject moves me and it is often not until much later that I understand its relevance to my life. I realise whether I appear in the photograph personally or not, my photographs are all self-portraits.

As with dance, I would like my photographs to touch the viewer at a sensitive level, a level normally protected.

This exhibition has given me the opportunity to reflect upon my life. To think about what I stand for now and the thread that leads from my past to the present.

At present I live in Berlin, a city that many Berliners refer to as an island. On this island of freedom surrounded by Communism, I am constantly aware of the forces of life, death and rebirth. Berlin is a living testament: a Pheonix rising from its own ashes.

My life can be described as a balancing act. I work to give equal attention to my dualities. I will not let go of the ancient side for the modern, nor do I mind jumping in front of and behind the camera. The key to maintaining balance lies in my ability to be true to the promise of Pandora.

Untitled photograph

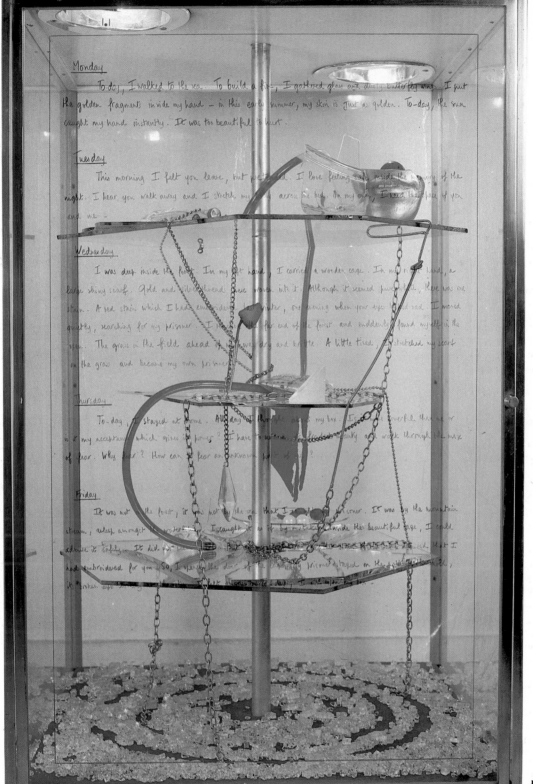

Janine Lajudie
Pandora's Diary
Mixed media

Jane Lewis
Mausoleum
Watercolour, 20 x 28 ins.

Joanna Woodward
The Milkmaid's Refusal
Mixed media

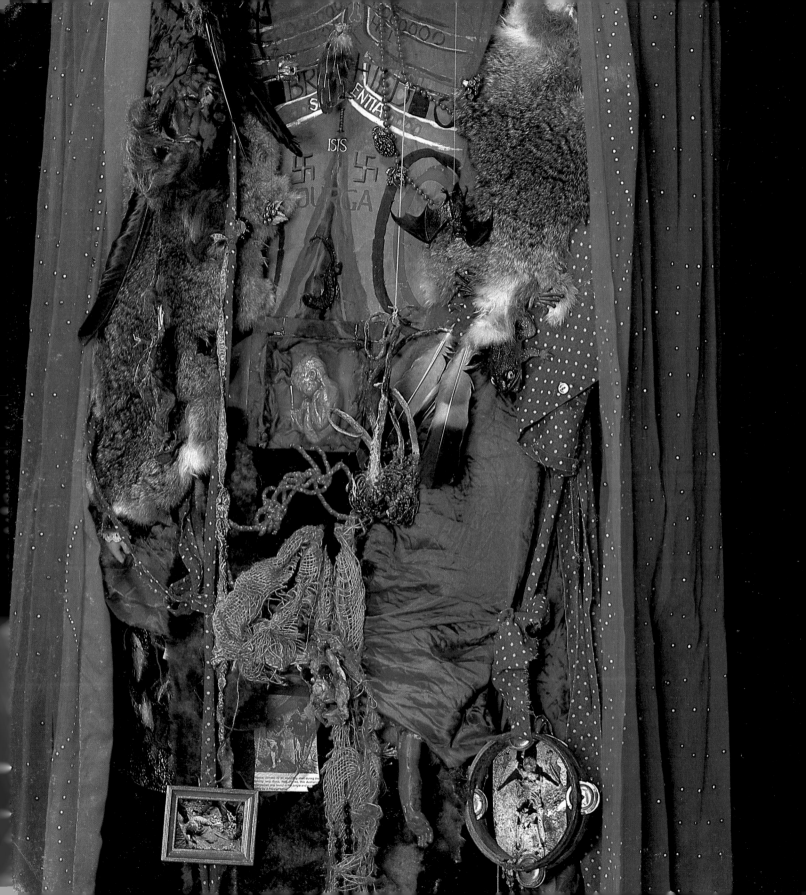

Linda Black

Linda Black

Helen Ganly
Pandora
(detail)

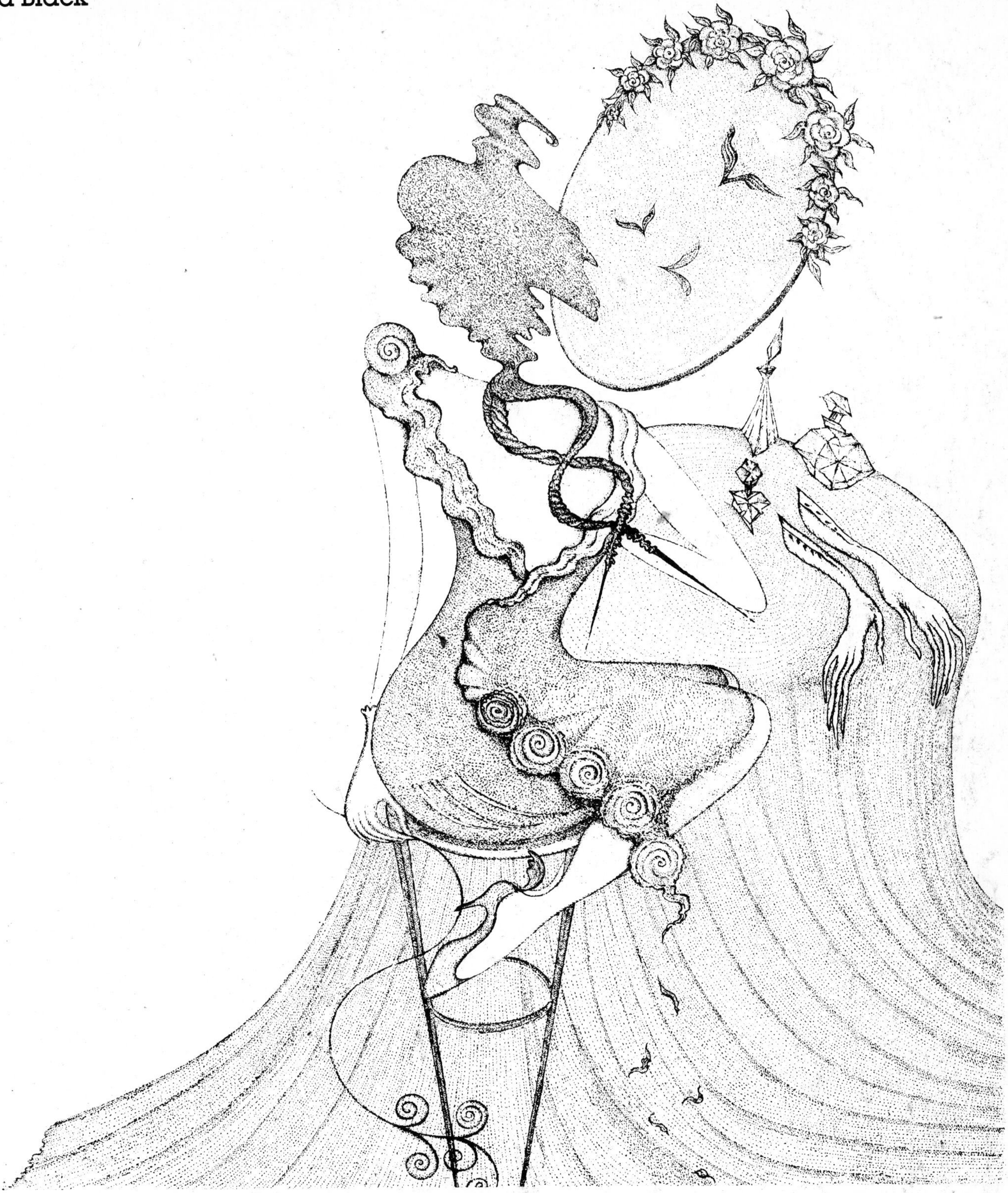

Dressing Table
Etching

Linda Black

**The women in my pictures are
many things.
– they are not to be pinned down.
They are mysterious, troubled,
alone, never safe, sometimes sexy,
sometimes demure, caught in a
web. They are victims, yet at the
same time they have a strength
and power that should not be
underestimated.
Their world is a sinister and
precarious place to be. There are
many beautiful things to be found
in it, but there is always something
nasty lurking around the corner,
something ominous and fore-
boding.
Women are made to feel a guilt
and responsibility for what it is
that troubles them – they are
caught in a predicament. Pandora
opened the box but she did not
create the troubles. Now that the
box is open the contents are all
around. The world is the box.**

I began etching in the final term of
my last year at Leeds Art College, just
by chance. At that time my ideas were
not at all worked out. Detail was of
primary importance, composition was
arbitrary. I began drawing with no
idea of my finished picture at all. My
plate was etched in one go. It was an
exciting way to work. For a while I
taught art in schools, using my way of
drawing as a starting point for
reluctant pupils, many of whom were
unable to express themselves visually,
feeling that art was restricted only to
those who could draw in the traditional sense. Many surprised themselves by their own ability. Whether
they could 'draw' or not didn't matter
to me. I was more interested in their
ideas – techniques were secondary. I
felt (feel) drawing to be a starting
point from which anything is possible.
During these years I did none of
my own work. (I often thought about it
and felt bad but all my energies went
into teaching). It was only after my
first child was born that I began
etching again. I discovered the local
Adult Education Institute and for the
next couple of years spent only one
evening a week during term time at
an evening class. That was eight years

**Ribbons
Etching
6 x 5 ins.**

ago and I now have three children.
They have given me great strength –
they have proved to me that I am an
artist, that despite great obstacles I am
able to continue drawing. For me the
greatest difficulty in being an artist
and a mother is finding time to pursue
my ideas. My loyalties are divided
between home and work, between
being an artist and a mother. Often it
is easier to give in and stop working,
but I have found it essential for my
self-respect not to. It has taken a lot of
effort and organization to produce the
small amount of work I have produced
during these years. Time for drawing
is very limited.

Recently my approach to my work
has changed. I now deliberate far
more over composition and even work
out my drawings very roughly before-
hand. Before, the excitement was in
not knowing what my ideas were, in
being surprised by what appeared. It
was as though my ideas evolved on
their own, almost without my intervention. Now I am more conscious of
them – I know (to some extent) what I
want to draw.

In 1979 I wrote this about my work:
My drawings take place in the same
world – a world which is sometimes a
void – empty and desolate with just a
piece of rag blown by the wind. Often,
the people are lost, floating, searching
(as in real life) – alienated from themselves and from others. Life is tragic
and hopeless and happiness occurs on
isolated occasions – and then you can
dance for joy!

My recent pictures are all of women.
Though it seems to me that maybe
they are about to disappear – merge
into the background, become part of
the elements – they are the stuff the
world is made of. I don't usually
analyse my ideas – if I do too much I
might frighten them away.

Birds of Prey
Etching
7 x 5½ ins.

Linda Black

Catherine McWilliams

Catherine McWilliams

Belfast College of Art was, in 1960 a very dull and uninspiring establishment. It was organized like a school with timetabled classes which included drawing from plaster reproductions of antique sculpture. The staff, with the exception of one embroidery tutor, was all male. Teaching was minimal and little attention was paid to twentieth-century innovations. As far as the staff was concerned Cubism, Fauvism or Futurism may never have happened. In those early days of the 'Swinging Sixties' female students weren't permitted to wear trousers into college. A successful protest was organised by the students' union, but apart from that the union was ineffectual in college affairs. The overriding discimination at that time was an institutionalized one against Catholics and other forms of prejudice passed unnoticed or seemed of small matter.

I didn't begin to paint seriously until I left College. I remained in Northern Ireland and consequently the Troubles have often been reflected in my paintings. In a lot of my work during the seventies the landscape or background tended to be overpowering, something I was aware of and chose to emphasise. This resulted in giving a feeling of isolation to the figures, particularly those of women living in troubled areas of Belfast. I portrayed these women as passive individuals in a landscape of deprivation and violence.

Although Belfast is a grim industrial city it has a beautiful natural setting. Lying at the estuary of the River Lagan, it is dominated to the North and West by the Cavehill and Divis mountains, and to the South it stretches into drumlin country.

While this Irish landscape is present in most of my work, sometimes it symbolizes freedom and hope, at other times it takes on a sinister or claustrophobic quality. But the central and most important element in my work is the human form. In recent years I have produced images of women and men in society, often trapped by their

Woman with peace line
Acrylic collage on paper, 30 x 23 ins.

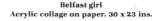

Belfast girl
Acrylic collage on paper, 30 x 23 ins.

environment; sometimes metamorphosing into bird or animal images, in a fantastical flight from reality; at other times striving to assert their individuality. One particularly important drawing of that time (1979) *A Woman's Place* was motivated not by the Troubles but by the thought of any woman who feels she has become almost 'invisible', only regarded as someone's wife or mother. In the drawing a female form merges with a window frame, becoming part of the furniture of the house, while in a second female figure I tried to convey a sense of movement; the woman asserting herself, becoming an individual, moving out of, away from 'A Woman's Place'. Very often the hopelessness of the Northern Ireland situation led me to look inward at my own family. As a result of this I produced a number of paintings based on my children where I tried to express the ephemeral quality of Innocence in a dangerous society.

It was this notion of Innocence that I incorporated into my first painting based on the myth of Pandora's Box. In *Girl with Birds and Dying Flowers* the innocent and youthful Hope is threatened by menacing birds and decaying flowers. In other representations of Pandora I am also concerned with innocence or hope but combined with life in Northern Ireland. In *Woman with Peace Line* the constant presence of armed forces is seen not only in the camouflaged image of Belfast's Cavehill, but in the existence of the Peace Line, the figure is woven with hopeful colours which break away into the background. In *Belfast Girl* the figure is seen as a survivor emerging from Belfast's debris. The now commonplace security barriers which surround Belfast appear to trap the figure in *Woman and Security Barriers* but this is countered by the pale tones of fragmented colour which link the woman's head with a distant hopeful landscape.

In *Irish Landscape I* Pandora has become part of the hopeful landscape. While in *Irish Landscape II* she seems trapped in the greyness and violence of Belfast, but this is alleviated by the

Woman with security barrier
Oil on canvas, 26 x 36 ins.

hopeful colours in the figure which
strive to move out of the greyness to
link with similar colours of a nearby
landscape.

In *Cavehill and Figures* Pandora is
no longer a passive being; although
part of the landscape of Cavehill, she
is throwing off the colours of Northern
Ireland conflict, and striving to push
aside 'the woes and miseries of the
world.'

Catherine McWilliams

Louise Baker

Boxes have always fascinated me. My grandparents and mother all had wooden chests in which were kept documents, photographs and other momentoes – buttons from uniforms; feathers; old pens; letters tied together with tape; the diary of a great-great-uncle; a wooden section from a World War I aircraft wing; a small paper folder containing a dozen or so small stones, rubies, saphires and topazes removed from their gold settings during the 30s depression; foreign coins and a tiny red seed which opened to reveal a minute carved ivory elephant. Part of their fascination was of course that I was not supposed to play with them. They were forbidden treasure caskets to be sorted through, all the items taken out laid in rows and then replaced in their former

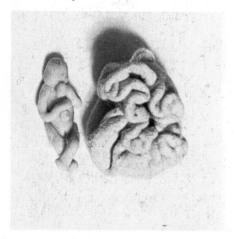

positions. I am still unable to see a box in a shop or auction room without opening it and have an acute sense of disappointment if it proves to be empty. I remember with a sense of loss the jumbled dusty displays of artefacts in glass cases in the provincial museums I visited as a child. I cannot feel the same sense of discovery in today's sanitized scientifically arranged displays. The image of boxes as essential items in life was reinforced during the nine years I taught in northern Nigeria. The wives' quarters I visited always contained at least one decorated metal trunk for each women and in it she would keep her most valuable belongings, wrapper lengths

and other clothing as well as jewellery, safe from the ravages of sand and termites. The market places were a treasure trove of containers made from red dyed goat skins, cigarette and evaporated milk tins, as well as the more expected brass sheet or wood. Different shaped containers had different functions and could be for antimony or snuff, amulets, balms or the Quoran. The sculptural mud architecture of the north was reminiscant of boxes with hidden compartments, secret rooms off dark passageways that contained some unexpected treasure – a vast brass bed or a wall

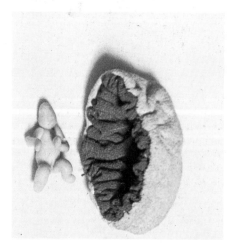

hidden by shelf after shelf of decorated enamel or brass cooking pots, part of the bride price, that would never be used.

I consider the Pandora's Box myth on a par with the Garden of Eden myth, that is, as part of the denegation of women in the overthrow of a matriarchal and matrilineal society by a patriarchal one, as part of the suppression of an Earth Mother Goddess by a Father God. It would have been essential for the first patriarchs to have attained some new knowledge in order for them to do this. I have envisaged Pandora as the woman who disclosed this knowledge to men which gave them the realization of their importance in the creation of life. Women's power was in their knowledge of life and growth both in the animal and plant world. By a series of taboos men could have been prevented from knowing or understanding the connection between intercourse, menstruation, pregnancy and birth both in humans and in the domestic animals they herded. Women as agriculturalists with their knowledge of the connection between seasonal events, the growing of crops and the appearance of fruits would have made them the most powerful element in society.

The box I have constructed shows women as the goddesses, the creators and harvesters, the holders of knowledge. Like all the work I am able to do at the moment, it was made within two very limiting constraints, lack of time and total lack of money. As a 37 year old 'unemployed' married women with a three-year-old daughter time is the most precious commodity. As in most non-city areas, child care facilities are extremely limited. During any one week I have three three-hour sessions when I am free to work during the daytime. I can count on another twenty-one hours a week if I work for three hours every night after my daughter has gone to bed. Because of this and the financial considerations I work small, making individual components that can be built up over many months to make a complete work. All the

Details of "Pandora's Box"

materials I use are those bought during the nine years I was teaching and lecturing in West Africa.

That this exhibition should contain work only by women is valid in that these patriarchal myths still govern the social mores of the present time and women need a forum in which to express their ideas. Any woman artist working now, whatever her own family and religous background, will have been reared in an obsessively male society. Her secondary education will have taken place in a system which positively discriminated against girls and higher education will have taken place in institutions run almost exclusively by men.

Louise Baker

prior to this exhibition, I did not know any women artists, and the contemporary shows I saw were self-referential, and could only have appealed to an educated elite. In a recent exhibition of current art at the Tate, of two hundred artists shown, eight were women.

College intake is approximately fifty percent female, yet posts in art education are five percent female, decreasing at higher levels. The argument that women do not want or are unable to do this kind of work, is no justification. In arts administration the situation improves, especially in the regions. However, in terms of practising artists applying for grants, men are about ten times more likely to succeed than women.

The myth of Pandora, and that of Eve, have always appeared to be condemning women twice: claiming that she incited others to do evil and is therefore guilty, but powerless; or, as in the case of Mary, exalted, but not human. These concepts must in part account for the religious and political notions which aid the fear and mistrust of female imagination and inspiration that have prevented women from achieving equality.

Equality has been understood theoretically, although not practised in many areas. However, the arts have a notion of 'quality' which excuses all forms of discrimination on the basis that success denotes merit, and if unsuccessful, the work is undeserving. Almost every living artist would disagree, yet the idea is universally accepted. The pursuit of the arts generally involves an unemployed majority. The visual arts in particular support this as a means of protecting the investment in the few artists who succeed. It is not remarkable in a society where visual images of all kinds are freely available, that fine art is only bought, and mostly seen, by a wealthy elite, and that which succeeds conforms to prevailing fashions and often functions as decor. The result is a gap between the public and the art establishment which some artists have

been trying to breach by working in areas outside the galleries, and concerning themselves with current issues. There is now an unfortunate division between 'fine art' and 'community' art, the two seem mutually exclusive for those who organise them, although not for the participants who are interested in combining the best aspects of each. Generally, I think women are more able to accept the dichotomy between 'fine' and 'community' art than men. There are two reasons for this, firstly, they are trained to be flexible, to unite rather than divide in social situations. Secondly, their career expectations are much less defined than men's. It seems they are interested in working for it's own sake, and hope for success while men often construct work which is designed to fit the prevailing taste, and expect to have it shown.

When making the initial selection for *Pandora's Box*, I discovered that my own preconceptions for looking at work were traditional in both attitude and language, using terms such as 'strong' for work I liked, and favouring a very academic approach, despite my feminist thinking in other areas, especially teaching. It took some time for me to overcome this bias, helped by the variety of work submitted. Seeing the work of the initial two hundred effected this change.

Women artists do have certain problems not shared by men. As in all fields, they are, by their conditioning, more readily distracted by others. This difficulty does not indicate a lack of concentration, but rather a breadth of vision which incorporates human needs, however trivial, with their personal aims. The result is an ability to both understand and communicate in diverse ways, which consciously or not, is manifested in their work. They do not mystify for it's own sake, but seek to facilitate the general understanding of their concerns. Practically, many of the artists have mentioned 'guilt' associated with establishing a work situation where

they cannot be disturbed, or when they have not been able to use it well. Most are taking the major role in domestic and social responsibilities, even when their partner is in a position to do this. Women, it seems, will tailor their work to the available space and time, while men tend to do the opposite.

These differences are the result of early training, when girls are discouraged from self-absorbtion in imaginative pursuits, while boys are praised for it — a subtle check on female inspiration. Later, girls are encouraged to give priority to social duties above personal talents and ambitions. Many parents still see colleges as a means of occupying their daughters before they marry, and art colleges often select female students for reasons not related to their abilities, although students have effectively challenged this. The prevailing stereotype of the successful 'male' artist, is of a figure apart from the world, with a special 'talent' distancing him from society. Women are too fundamental to accept this; they have to communicate with all ages, and at many levels, so it is assumed that are less able to communicate visually. Most women artists have to overcome these predjudices before they achieve the confidence to seriously pursue their own careers.

In my work I have tried to visualise the relative positions of women in society; the 'guilt' felt by women induced by religion, education and the law. Working as a teacher I have realised that for ordinary women who are excluded from the mainstream of ideas, there is no equality. There are very few involved in the arts at any level, because art is totally devalued in their terms. My paintings are all concerned with the struggle of women to surmount the ideas and conventions which keep them at a distance from their objectives.

SO COMFORTING.

IT HAD SOMETHING TO DO WITH THE EBB AND FLOW.

SOMEHOW IT CUT THROUGH ALL THAT RHETORIC.

SHE WAS EXHILARATED, HER SEXUALITY REAFFIRMED!

A WOMAN! WHAT A WOMAN!

Washing Day
Mixed media

1. WASHING: Content

B: What does a woman desire?
A: er . . . er . . . er . . . a washing machine!
B: How many washing machines?
A: One, with a tumble dryer, . . or a spin dryer.
B: And how many pounds of washing should the washing machine hold?
A: 15.
B: 15!! Thats quite a big washing machine, how many times a week should she wash?
A: Once.
B: Just once a week?!
A: Clothes? – you mean her body or her clothes?
B: Ha, ha, ha, clothes.
A: What she does is gets them all together and separates the colours from the whites – and say you have two washes a week – that is if you haven't got any kids – the two washes being the colours and the whites . . .

B: What about your washing up clothes and towels and drying up towels . .?
A: They go in with the whites.
B: And sheets.
A: They go in with the whites.
B: And duvet covers.
A: They go in with the whites.
B: So she's just going to wash one day a week, you don't think she would get obsessed and want to wash every single day because . . .
A: What you do is every day you kind of put things in the washing machine, to be washed, say, on Wednesday . . .
B: But you would have it filled up in, like, two days and then you'd just . .
A: NO – you wouldn't not in just two days . . .
B: . . . get whole n'other pile
A: No you wouldn't. You'd just wait till it filled up and then just turn it on so you don't even have to worry about organising it, you just shove it in and turn it on, and then take it all out.

B: Er . . where would you put it?
A: Put what?
B: The washing machine.
A: Down next to the cooker.
B: Is there a space?
A: Yes.
B: What a special place for it? But then you have to take your clothes down from the bedroom or the bathroom to the . . .
A: SO . . . . .?
B: But its such a . . .
A: No thats no problem, not compared to . . .
B: So when you have . . .
A: Going to the launderette.
B: . . your, your after your breakfast or something you just take them in put them there.
A: Yeah. . . .
B: Yeah. . . .
A: I think it'd be good.
B: With a tumble dryer its good.

2. READING: point of view

'No one notices it until it isn't done – we notice the unmade bed – not the scrubbed and polished floor. Invisible, repetitive, exhausting, unproductive, uncreative – these are the adjectives which most perfectly capture the nature of housework. The new consciousness associated with the contemporary women's movement has encouraged increasing numbers of women to demand that their men provide some relief from this drudgery. Already more men have begun to assist their partners around the house, some of them even devoting equal time to household chores. But how many of these men have liberated themselves from the assumption that housework is 'womens' work'? How many of them would not characterise their housecleaning activities as 'helping' their women partners? If it were at all possible simultaneously to liquidate the idea that housework is women's work and to redistribute it equally to men and women alike, would this constitute a satisfactory solution?

Yet female domestic labour has not always been what it is today, for like all social phenomena, housework is a fluid product of human history. Colonial (American) women were not 'house-cleaners' or 'housekeepers' but rather fully-fledged and accomplished workers within the home-based economy. Not only did they manufacture most of the products required by their families, they were also the guardians of their families and their communities' health. But by the end of the century there became more apparent the fundamental, structural, separation between the domestic home economy and the profit orientated economy of capitalism. Since housework does not generate profit, domestic labour was naturally defined as an inferior form of work as compared to capitalist wage labour. In advanced capitalist societies the service-orientated domestic labour of housewives, who can seldom produce tangible evidence of their work, diminishes the social status of women in general. When all is said and done,

the housewife according to bourgeois ideology is, quite simply, her husband's life long servant.

There are movements in a number of capitalist – countries their main concern being that of the housewife. Having reached the conclusion that housework is degrading and oppressive, primarily because it is unpaid labour, this movement has raised the demand for wages. A weekly government paycheck, it's activists argue, is the key to improving the housewife's status and the position in general. The theoretical origins of the Wages for Housework Movement can easily be found in an essay by Mariarosa Dalla Costa entitled 'Women and the Subversion of the Community'. In this paper she argues for a redefinition of housework based on her thesis that the private character of household services is actually an illusion. The housewife, she insists, only appears to be ministering to the private needs of her husband and children, for the real beneficiaries of her services are her husband's present employer and the future employers of her children.

'The idea of a pay check for housewives would probably sound quite attractive to many women. But the attraction would probably be short lived. For how many of those women would actually be willing to reconcile themselves to deadening, never-ending household tasks, all for the sake of a wage? Would a wage alter the fact, as Lenin said, that . . .

'. . . petty house work crushes, strangles, stultifies and degrades the woman, chains her to the kitchen and to the nursery, and wastes her labour on barbarously unproductive, petty, nerve-racking, stultifying and crushing drudgery.' It would seem that government paychecks for housewives would further legitimize this domestic slavery. What the Wages for Housework Movement want, however, in the long run is jobs and generally available, affordable, public child care.

The abolition of housework as the private responsibility of individual women is clearly a strategic goal of womens liberation. But the social-

isation of housework including meal preparation and child care – presupposes an end to the profit – motives reign over the economy. The only significant steps towards ending domestic slavery have in fact been taken in the existing socialist countries. Working women, therefore, have special and vital interest in the struggle for socialism. Moreover, under capitalism, campaigns for institutions such as subsidized public child care, contain an explosive revolutionary potential. This strategy calls into question the validity of monopoly capitalism and must ultimately point in the direction of socialism . . .'

To talk about one's own artwork, it is necessary to examine and explain one's own thought processes; something I find difficult to do.

I can see it clearly in visual form. It's not a linear, orderly thing. Rather like a point, moving through space, that reaches out and grabs all passing thought forms, pulling them into itself. Once inside, chaos reigns. All thoughts jostle for supremacy. They become like orphans who have forgotten their heritage and are desparately seeking their security in a new home. The mind is one, the thoughts are many, sanity verges on defeat. But now the situation changes. The mind rallies and separates into an army of thousands. These surround and besiege each thought, until it surrenders, and in the process yields whatever secrets it may possess. Each thought then becomes a part of the constantly shifting, and sifting process of the mind, separating here, pairing there, forming clusters of related, though often apparently unrelated, ideas. Eventually all becomes homogenous, and like the sea, is calm in it's deepest parts but breaks into waves as it meets the shore of another person's mind. Sometimes the meeting is gentle, sliding along a sandy beach. At other times, the waves hit a rocky crag and rebound with fierce abandon. When the stars are inharmonious, storms arise at sea, and can even become a hurricane, with a will to destroy any unyielding object in it's path.

If I were able to join each related particle within my mind by colored strings, the overlapping complexity would increase until there was nothing but black. At this point the mind goes into a spin, black becomes white, and a vision appears as though on a screen. One image gives way to another in rapid succession. A graphic shorthand is necessary to record frames in a moving picture. A shorthand intelligible to none but myself, it serves as a reminder rather than a plan.

It is then that the real work begins: that of unravelling the strings and choosing the image that will be produced. Because the type of work I do is particularly time-consuming, I

She arrived with a box tucked under her arm. Imprisoned in it were a scorpion, a serpent. An eagle and a dove. No one told her that she must not open the box, and so she did. But when she lifted the lid, the eagle gave her a haughty glare and flew away searching for the highest peak; the scorpion stung her with it's tail and scurried off to live in the desert; the serpent whispered in her ear then bit her hand and slithered off into the marshland. The only creature that remained was a small white dove. It seemed to be fatally wounded by the activity of the other three. She took it upon herself to stay by the box nursing the dove back to health. The dove became her closest companion, and soon she began to fear that once able to fly again the dove would leave her. So she climbed into the box herself and shut the lid so neither could escape. It was very dark inside the box. after several centuries of this existence, she was no longer sure of who she was or what she was doing.

Like the Phoenix She Arose
Mixed media, 12 x 22 x 18 ins.

She no longer remembered how she came to be in the box. She waits now. The dove and she have long since ceased to be separate. She and it are one. She waits and hopes that there is another one Without fear – someone who will open the box.

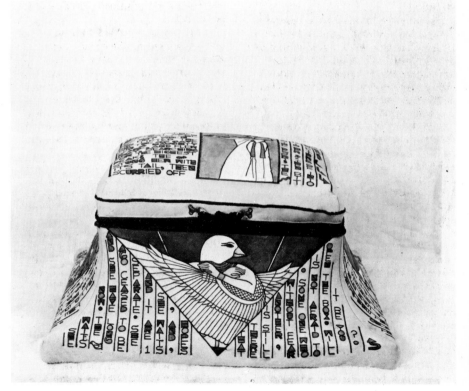

am normally faced with the necessity of choosing only one of many equally deserving images, before I am compelled to move on. I always try to work on a piece that is a challenge in some way, from which I can learn something new in technique. The final choice must also take account of limitations of time and space and the inevitable financial considerations.

Eventually, the tails of all the colored strings become incorporated in some way, perhaps as a symbolic detail culled from psychology, astrology, philosophy, esoteric beliefs. They're not important in themselves, but may add an extra dimension for people interested in those things.

My natural way of working is a cyclic process. I first need time to be alone, at least three days cut off from the world. By the end of a week of solitude, I'm usually working very well. Once into this mode, I find it almost impossible to communicate verbally with other people: nor do I particularly want to. It's as though nothing of importance exists outside myself and my work. I find it easy to work intensively for twenty hours a day – almost impossible not to. Food and sleep become unimportant as I become all but sustained by the working process. Not surprisingly, I come out of these times feeling completely drained and exhausted; wanting first to sleep for days and then return to socializing, and just being lazy.

Unfortunately, life does not easily accomodate this way of working. Outside pressures combine to enforce a conventional routine. For me, such a regime seems better to suit those tasks which are better done while half asleep. Or is it just that certain jobs and everyday routine put me to sleep, like the constant drone of a machine?

When it comes to movement and pose, the emotional content of figures – I never use a model, but use myself instead. I try to invoke the feelings within myself by setting up a drama, a story in my head – a kind of dialogue. I usually go through several scenes, acting out all the roles, until I find the one that feels right. Then I move around, using whatever I've learned

from dance, T'ai Chi, or other physical disciplines. I move until I come to the same feeling that I arrived at through the play acting. If I can imagine some music, it is a help, but I'm not very musical so this rarely happens. I carry on making the movements smaller and stiller, until they come to a halt. I then practice this again and again, until I can memorize the pose and feel the dialogue in my body.

From here, I set about finding things – fabrics, paints, wood, wire, whatever I need. I try to approach it like a game that children play. A scavenger hunt, that may lead me almost anywhere. Usually, shopping really bores me.

All too often, practical considerations intervene in the creative process. Take for instance, the bird-woman in the egyptian box. I really wanted her to fly. But even after many long talks with her, and consultations with a friendly engineer, she simply refused to totally comply. Or rather, she patiently explained that she would fly out, quite happily, but then, she would be most unlikely to return to repeat the performance for the next person who chose to open the box. So in the end, it had to be a compromise. Oh yes, I neglected to say, I always talk to my work.

Once a work gets beyond a certain stage, it's no longer so dependent on me, and starts, like any child, to develop a mind of it's own. It often disagrees with my own intellectual judgement, and we spend a lot of time negotiating. Sometimes I can begin to loose sight of my original goal. Well-meaning friends make suggestions to me. My own mind starts thinking of other things. But usually the work knows who or what it wants to be, and asserts its influence until I give in and do what it says. If I'm able to be alone with my work the relationship is congenial. Otherwise, I do my best to overlook and generally cope with, the sometimes aggressive impatience with which a work demands to be finished. To be fair, the work equally overlooks a bit of clumsyness on my part and so we normally end up as friends.

Although once through the process, I tend to verge on being a critical

perfectionist, and so continually find fault with every piece. A dissatisfaction which, like all things, has its good and bad side.

The mythology of Pandora once looked into, was almost overwhelming. The connections were so profuse that at times it seemed my system was overloaded and about to blow a fuse. Finally, I decided on a series of 4 boxes.

The idea of the boxes, was drawn from associations and interpretations of the myth by way of the mental processes described earlier. Basically I began in an individual and Jungian sense to see the box in terms of inside and outside – the person and his/her anima/

She was once the oracle of the Greeks – the source of all gifts to mankind fostered by fate, the circle turned, man turned to man in love and hate, left to govern the real world. He quickly found a place for her but then she . . . . .

Venus Trapped like a Fly
Mixed media, 34 ins. high

animus. **This got mixed up with ideas about the collective unconscious and the possibility of a shadow side of a civilization or particular point in time. One of the things that struck me about the myth itself, was that each successive generation and civilisation, subtly changed the myth to suit their own time. And so Pandora changed from beneficial earth mother/goddess, to the Pandora we know today. It seemed to chart the history of male attitudes to woman, and in a Jungian sense, to the feminine aspects of himself and his society.**

Rather than rely on what I'll call 'book history', as a basis or underlying inspiration, I drew upon my own recollections of past lives. As I can clearly remember small clusters of lives during the egyptian, classical and medieval european periods, I chose these as symbolic phases or turning points in attitude toward the female/feminine.

I wanted to use series of boxes to demonstrate this in some way; to weave the myth, my personal history, and the changing civilizations together in such a way that the inside of one, became the outside of the next. I hoped that the progression, although personal to me, would also show the history of women, of the feminine.

The fourth box represents the present and future computer age. We are all faced with the dilema of Pandora. Whether or not to open the box and face ourselves. As a society, we have already been overwhelmed by our curiosity. We have opened many boxes and no matter what horrors have emerged, we continually retain the hope that there will be something good at the bottom of it all.

A very simplified version of history might read: The early Egyptians believed in transformation; that man was on earth to learn to control his own destiny, even beyond the grave. The gods each had their positive and negative aspects, and were seen as inspiration and warning. Human kind aspired to be as gods. All paths to the light were accepted.

As the light passed to the Greeks, it became more and more deeply embedded in the sensual, physical aspects of life. The seat of intelligence moved from the heart to the head. Man began to judge himself and his fellow with logic rather than love. Now, the gods controlled the fate of man, and struggled amongst themselves. And it seemed as though the gods aspired to be like man.

It was during the classical period that the history of humankind finally split into the history of man, and the parallel but slightly different history of woman. That is why I write here of the history of man, while my work is concerned with the history of woman.

I thought the message of Jesus was to return to the purity of earlier times. But instead, Christianity continued the downward descent of man. While the greek loved the body, perhaps too much; the Christian was taught to despise his. Condemned as a sinner by his mere birth, he could no longer ask a friendly god to intervene. The one and only god, spoke only with the priest. Only one religion was to be tolerated. Even God was separated into 3, with his fourth and completing part sent to reside in hell, and from there continue the persecution of man.

Man, now separated from his soul, his body, his god, and his fellow man, divised ways to separate himself from his sense of achievement in work and life, through industrialization and the breakdown of community life. Through education, even the family was separated from itself. The computer age threatens to sever the link between man and his mind, between man and any sense of his own identity. His technology is able to separate him from the earth, by travel or destruction.

Will the final outcome be that man completely disappears from the face of the earth? Or, will he come full circle, to another kind of golden age? And where does that leave woman? **Perhaps when man sees that a machine can be more intelligent and useful than he; that in all the ways that he considers himself superior to woman, he can easily be bettered by technology then**

will he begin to appreciate the feminine. Then will the histories of man and woman link up again.

Because I like stories, and it is mainly the job of women to tell stories to their children, I wrote a story for each box; as a complimentary part of the visual rather than as explanation. Unlike most stories, they begin with SHE. They have no ending: for the story continues today.

She was held by feverish devotion. Pristine in gratitude for all the gifts she gave, humble and self-sacrificing, she dressed in sackcloth so that others could wear the cloth of gold. Eventually, her only option illuminated her life. Whereupon she . . .

The Female Pope
Mixed media, 21 x 35 x 5 ins.

Mouse Katz

Joan Wakelin

I am a photojournalist.
I believe in the 'human condition'.
Gender has no meaning in a working capacity.
I am a photographer.
I am totally involved.
I am religious but have no religion.
I believe in laughing and crying.
I believe in compassion.
I believe my pictures explain.

I was born in the North and had an orthodox up-bringing. Then came a scholarship to the local Grammar school, but I was persuaded by my parents to leave early, and started work in the photographic section of Aero Engine Research Laboratory of Shell Mex, Chester. Married young. I had two children and eventually settled in a small village in Berkshire. If some of my time and enthusiasm was spared for sport (tennis and sailing), nonetheless photography came first.

I have had many one-woman shows in Britain and in such places as Colombo and Singapore – at present I am touring and lecturing in Australasia for a year, and I am planning a future programme in India. 'Women's Images of Men' was the first time I had been involved in a mixed-media exhibition, and I found meeting other women artists a stimulating experience, as was the inter-play of ideas and feelings.

For me a new project was born on a visit to Greenham Common for the memorable December 12th demonstration, when uncountable numbers of women linked hands in protest,

**Greenham Common
Photograph**

with the support of thousands of others. It was an exciting and stimulating day, that led to innumerable photographs from which the present work was generated.

But with the aftermath of 12th December, and subsequent return visits to Greenham, came a welter of searching questions. What were my views regarding the camp, the political situation, feminism; where did I stand? I was aware of the difficulty facing most artists of how to perceive and scrutinise the facets of life one is interpreting, without being drawn into them. To remain objective, yet still feel the sensations within, is the problem known to every creative worker. Nor am I one for titles and roles: I hope that a way of independently looking at life and recording it shows in the work I do. Am I a 'feminist'? – perhaps of a kind, but to be contained in a single category is not the answer, for as other artists know it can be narrowing and limiting to the prejudices of the creative role.

Joan Wakelin

The pictures are part of some nine months' work. I hope in looking at them you will put aside for the moment your own political views and see them for their instrinsic quality. The subject was chosen not only because it was on my doorstep, but because it is extremely relevant to the present day. I would say that the pictures reflect in many ways the title of the show 'Pandora's Box' – a man's world and the woman let the evil out. There are no poses here. No wizzy dark room techniques. No tricks of Fleet Street. Rather a blend of skills that gives our eye something meditative, challenging and revealing.

The pictures should explain: otherwise I have failed to communicate.

Greenham Common
Photograph

Marisa Rueda
Akewa's Road to Freedom
Ceramic figure

Joan Wakelin

Hilary Rosen
Hope had golden wings, 1983
Charcoal, ink and watercolour, 60 x 60 ins.

Maria Chevska
In the Sad Backyard Hope flies, 1982
Oil on canvas, 60 x 48 ins.

Mary McGowan
Prometheus & Pandora
Oil on canvas, 30 x 40 ins.

Janine Lajudie

I have been able to work on the myth of Pandora's Box because it was intriguing for me, a woman of the Twentieth Century, to see how I would approach it. I did so honestly, but allowing a minimum of information to sink into my mind. I treated it as a 'myth'. That is, for me, something one hears about, something vague, something overheard – one of those fascinating unimportant details which sticks 'at the back of one's mind'. I did not feel that I needed to research. I tried to react with innocence to a very old, worn out subject.

As a woman, it is difficult not to take into account 'feminist' issues. The fact that Pandora was created by the Gods to be responsible for the evils of the world is obviously a gloomy and very diminishing image of the first woman. This first reading of the myth left me feeling angry and wondering how different societies had integrated this myth. In this same reading, women are also responsible for hope – a more gratifying image although a somewhat puzzling afterthought. While questioning the social importance of the myth, a second reading became apparent, leaving me quite confused. This second reading absolves Pandora of any fault, as the real responsibility belongs to the superhuman force which created her, the box and even her action. This leaves her as a pathetic puppet likely to be forgiven, patted on the head and totally insignificant. All of a sudden the theme to study seemed to be the reasons why a superhuman power would create suffering amongst humans. This for me was irrelevant as there is no such power.

At a loss, I carried on working, simply letting the presence of this myth infiltrate the very close atmosphere of my studio and slowly a third reading started to take shape, creating a very different vision of this woman – a woman faced with a temptation, an interdiction – a woman having to make an irreversible decision. I kept thinking of another more recent myth 'Blue Beard' where a woman is refused access to a past – to the inner world of her husband's life – but more simply access to a room, to a key.

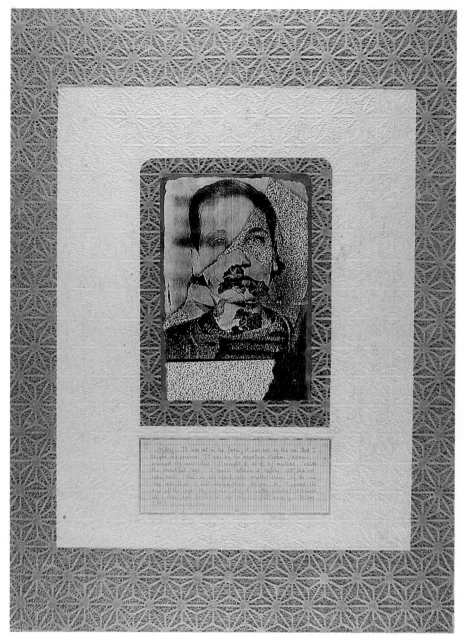

Pandora's Diary – Friday
Mixed media

Janine Lajudie

So, I started looking for a lockable box. Pandora having joined our dinner table conversations, the search for the box became a constant preoccupation. The right box was found, bought and stood in the middle of my room occupying a very large space. After months of hesitation and doubts as to whether I could do a work which was honest to the theme and to me, it seemed to take form and also meaning. **I see Pandora as a woman acting freely and breaking a rule, that is 'opening the box', in full knowledge and in full control of her action; therefore 'opening a transparent box'.**
It is not a forbidden box that Pandora opens in an uncontrolled fit of curiosity. It is an unknown dimension which she decides to explore. What could this unknown dimension be but part of oneself which, undiscovered appears as a dormant volcano and, discovered, threatens to create chaos. In other words, another dimension which imposes the need for a redefinition of oneself. The only possible one seemed the mountains of our dreams, our fears, our hidden desires, our fantasies...
Suddenly I felt very close to the myth of Pandora, very close to this woman ready to transgress – freeing herself from conventions, from an accepted knowledge of herself in order to look deeper; leaving behind a secure, predetermined existence but not necessarily leaving a structured way of thinking – rather building upon it, using its strength to go further. In this way, hope in the ancient myth becomes logical, an expectable item to be found at the bottom of the box. As for me, hope is an inherent part of the wish to go forward.

Some people have asked why there is no feeling of guilt in my interpretation of Pandora's Box. Guilt appearing as a possible consequence of making such an irreversible act. I cannot reconcile a fully aware, meant action: 'Today I will open my box', and a subsequent 'What did I do? . . . Why did I do

it? . . . I should not have done this . . .'. These are totally contradictory for me. The emotion that I associate with taking such a decision is much more one of fear; fear of the unknown, fear of oneself, fear that the search for a deeper self might just lead to a shattered present self and no new self.

I feel that I should say at least a few words about the visual works themselves. One is a transparent, lockable box. When I think back it appears that this piece of work grew alongside my questioning of the myth. It grew while trying to achieve a crystal clear quality. The five two-dimensional pieces, which I see as one work, came afterwards when the search for the meaning of the myth was over. All along, I kept thinking that if such a woman had really existed it would be fascinating to have documents of what she felt and thought at the time. So, I wrote my own diary of the few days leading to the day when Pandora decided to open the box. The words were written on the door of the box as a final stamp that Pandora was unlocking the box in full understanding of her action. Words have for me a power of their own. They are therefore a very important part of my work. This may be why the fragment of diary led to the other where the need for a box was no longer important.

Apart from the problem of the relevance of the myth to me and to the world I live in, and the problem of my own honesty within the theme, I had to face another question. Is there a reason for a women's show? Does it make a difference? My feelings on these questions are numerous. Part of me feels a strong solidarity with other woman artists. Part of me feels a solidarity with all artists. I know that to be an artist is a long and difficult struggle and that in any field society asks more of women before recognising them as equals. I know that the search for a women's identity in a world which has been dominated for a long time by a men-oriented ideology, must be part of a woman artist's awareness. All the same, the answer to this search does not have to be the separating of men from women. This

could tend to create an image of confrontation – one against the other – Is a women's show a negative move, a form of voluntary segregation, a self-inflicted ghetto?

Before attempting to answer these questions I would like to say that I am completely aware that the role of the artist and art in society are of too great an importance to be easily ridiculed and therefore destroyed by infighting. But then I have been forced to witness so much infighting within the offered structures of the art world that I cannot see why purety should not, once more, be the virtue of women. Men have turned art into a saleable item. Anything in our society which can generate money becomes mixed up in a totally different world. The world of business. The distance between the artist's struggle and the whereabouts of the resulting work of art is so long to walk that it is easy to get waylaid. To organise a women's show, therefore, may not be the purest answer to the search for a women's identity but it is a privilege in which women are indulging. I would very much like to know who feels that they can cast the first stone?

An all-women show is a show removed from the reality of everyday life, but is this not precisely what art is also about? By removing chunks of reality and reorganising them visually, poetically and musically artists have changed our perception of the world. Hopefully they have contributed to improving the world. An all-woman show, by imposing a fairly brutal recognition of woman as artists, might have, in the long term, a socially positive effect. I do not see this as a rejection of men artists, nor even of the conventional art world, but more as an attempt to create a new road, an alternative.

I must also say that working with women has been a marvellous discovery. I do not want to fall into the trap of generalising from a few examples, but the women I have met in the course of this show have been incredibly helpful, sharing and honest. A rare treat in the art world.

Thinking more precisely of this show,

another point seems to be worth mentioning here. The theme explored is deeply relevant to women, to the way women perceive themselves and to the way they have been perceived through many societies. I, therefore, really look forward to seeing various women's interpretations of such a damaging myth, or of the need for such a myth. One must admit that between Pandora and Eve there is not much of a choice.

Finally one aspect of this show which interests me deeply is the unanswered question of women's imagery. Is there such a thing? Seeing together the works of many women on one single theme makes me wonder if there will be a feeling of unity. Will there be a repeated use of certain images, materials, colours, shapes taking up a symbolic value? Will, on the other hand, each woman artist stand alone as an individual. Is the notion of women's imagery another cosmetic used to hide a woman's individuality, or is it a reality stemming from much deeper roots?

The words which I wrote as a fragment of Pandora's diary were meant to be read and re-read at length. Often, in my work, words end in their frozen printed state leaving me with a longing feeling for the immediacy and the fugitiveness of spoken words, whether overheard or screamed. This time the words are those buried inside a diary where the act of writing is surrounded by absolute secrecy and an ephemeral quality. Tomorrow having erased today, the reader becomes a magical thief able to give life to words new abandoned.

Untitled

Janine Lajudie

Helen Ganly

I was born into a family of artists. My parents had met at art school; my grandfather had been an illustrator, as were his two brothers – one of whom was Heath Robinson. I drew from an early age and was writing and illustrating my own books from the age of four years old. I was fortunate in being encouraged by my parents. I was always drawing, won prizes at school and in local shows and when I was fourteen, won two national painting competitions. At seventeen, I won a scholarship to the Slade and left school early to take up the place. I think this positive reinforcement at an early age has helped me to cope with subsequent rejections and frustrations. I have vivid memories of the Slade but I was shy, straight from school and although I took in everything, I missed many opportunities through lack of confidence in myself. At art school, one develops a self-critical faculty. This can be a very painful and an inhibiting experience. Mystification can be used to confuse and undermine a young artist, but if the inner necessity to paint and draw or sculpt is powerful enough, it will continue through what for many students can be a daunting experience.

Over the past few years, I have become far more aware of myself as an artist who happens to be a woman and all that condition implies. To some extent this awareness has become a back ground to my work. Reading the work of British and American feminist art historians, I understand more deeply my own artistic legacy; how that has influenced me; the role that my student days at the Slade played in my development as an artist and personally; and also my professional role as an artist and teacher set against my domestic one. Those feminist art historians I have read have thus given me an historical context in which to think through my ideas; and I am sustained in my determination to continue working and surviving as an artist by the new feminist art history which has begun to set the record right, by re-

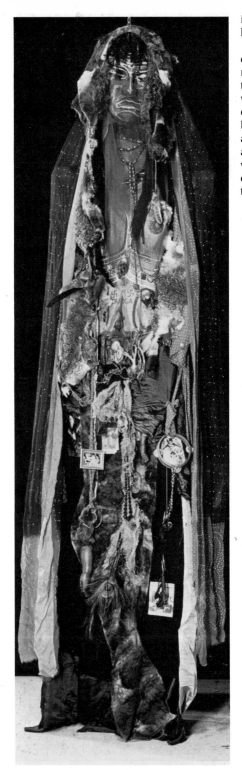

instating the female artist into art history.

I was always criticised for a lack of consistency of approach, but I have now come to terms with the fact that there are about four strands to my work which can all be worked on and expressed simultaneously. This may be a characteristic common to many artists. With regard to male or female art and imagery, I am doubtful as to whether one can make very clear distinctions. It seems to me that people tend to see what they want to see and conveniently ignore evidence which does not suit their particular argument. I know plenty of women artists whose work is non-figurative and large scale, whose work is strong and bold, as well as those whose work is small scale, delicate and illustrative. I also know men whose work is as varied as the women's. If anything, I feel that there is a greater freedom for women to slalom between different poles of expression, but I do not know whether this is due to the greater freedom to be found within their marginal position or whether it is due to specifically female characteristics.

Apart from one period of several years when I explored the formal problems of non-figurative painting, I have worked in a figurative idiom, and I have always responded to my environment by making objects, drawing or paintings as a way of making sense of my life and the world around me. A 'theme' is always sparked off by a visual stimulus, but as the theme is developed, taken up and creatively explored, using the means and scale appropriate to its requirements, other patterns of thought may develop and can take me off on a separate line of enquiry.

I did far less work when my children were young, but when they went to school, I did more – only this time unhampered by outside expectations, I was able to experiment more freely. I taught in an art school for ten years; I taught adult evening classes, in comprehensive schools, prep and public schools, in a mental hospital, a prison and I now teach in sixth form colleges. I am also a 'visiting artist' and lecturer to undergraduates in Oxford. In this latter role, I try to advise my students on how to survive as an artist. I believe that this has always been, and is now, very difficult and that those who have worked out different strategies for survival can give strength and support to others.

As I earn my living through teaching, I have complete freedom to do anything I like in my work, even if this sometimes means that certain projects are rejected by galleries as uncommercial. My freedom of expression and social mobility are essential to me as an artist.

At the moment, I share a small studio with a number of artists, men and women and I am a founder member of the Oxford Printmakers' Co-operative. Small scale work I do at home.

I am intrested in breaking down barriers between people in a positive way and show my work in shopping centres, libraries, housing estates, schools, hospitals, as well as in art galleries. I like to arrange exhibitions in which the spectators can become active participants because I believe that all human beings have untapped creative potential.

When I was selected as one of the artists to work on the theme of 'Pandora's Box', I was already deeply involved in a project of my own – which will be shown in London later this year. My work therefore reflects my concerns at this time.

I believe artists are part of society and therefore, whether they are aware of the fact or not, cannot avoid having their work read 'politically' even if their aims are not political. I know that my work not only reflects my involvement in my own community, it also reflects my working situation in the studio, my developing awareness of the women's movement and my personal situation. But as I have already stated, I have been expressing myself through a visual medium from the age of four, and that inner need is the over-riding factor.

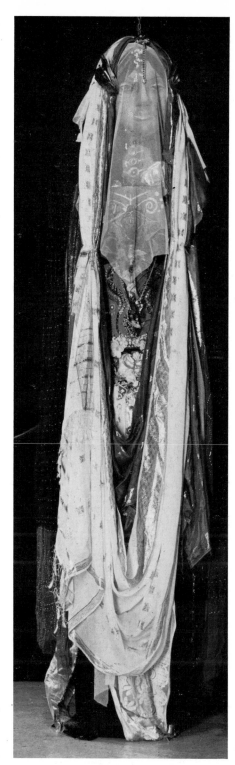

Pandora
Double-sided figure
Mixed media, 120 ins. high

I have researched the myth of Pandora very thoroughly and have notebooks packed with ideas and drawings, but I do not believe that symbols necessarily gain any power from being explained. I would rather each person experienced my work individually and primarily visually and took away with them images upon which to reflect. While researching this theme, three strands of thought became of prime importance to me. The ideas were developed using visual metaphors in varying degrees of complexity.

Helen Ganly

Jane Lewis

Jane Lewis

During my first year at art college, when the time arrived to make a decision about which subject I should take and to which college I should apply to take my degree (I was then, as occasionally even now, agonising over the question of whether I should determinedly pursue personal interests in my work and apply to study Fine Art, or to take the more practical course of opting for one of the 'applied arts') I sought the advice of one of my (male) tutors, who told me in no uncertain terms that, whatever else I did, I should avoid the Fine Arts. Of how many famous, or even successful women painters had I heard? The implication was that I would be wasting my and presumably the prospective college's time. This was more or less the extent of his advice.

I chose Fine Art.

There is not necessarily any discernible difference between the work of male and female artists, neither in appearance, application, nor even in approach – provided its content is bland, commonplace and not too deeply personal. As soon as the uniquely personal vision, the original observation of the uncommon artist emerges, the differences, albeit subtle, will usually be apparent. And to paraphrase Germaine Greer: the woman artist who is obviously so in a male society will usually fail unless she suppresses or disguises this aspect of herself.

As to discrimination against women as artists: I do not think I have encountered any direct discrimination. At one time I would have said I had experienced none whatsoever – but as time goes by and a distinct lack of interest in and difficulty in showing my work persists, I begin to suspect rather an unspoken, more insidious form of discrimination.

Women's work as artists will tend to be ignored more often than it is opposed.

Pandora
Watercolour, 25 x 20 ins.

At present I feel somewhat out on a limb; discontented with the bits and pieces of part-time teaching I have managed to acquire, yet unsure of which new direction I can take – if indeed there is an alternative.

I would like to have talked more about my work, but I think it is a very difficult thing indeed for a visual artist, at least an artist of my own persuasion, to make a written statement about her own work. As artists, we may feel compelled to vent political and/or social beliefs through our work. But sometimes I feel that the visual arts (with the exception perhaps of film) are not always the best media through which to express such ideas: there are surely certain ones which must be purely visual in concept and execution.

I have not always been particularly successful in capturing too rigidly defined an idea in a painting, print or drawing. Indeed, images seem to appear of their own free will, all too frequently reaching a quite unexpected conclusion. I prefer to avoid direct comment in my work. Though my imagery is usually strong, and may often appear to make some kind of direct statement, its intention is invariably at least a little obscure. I would like to think that my work creates rather a certain mood which might describe the contemporary human condition.

My work has often been given a feminist interpretation, and although I would not completely disagree, I would nevertheless not call the inclination overt. Feminism has very naturally, perhaps at times unconsciously, found its way into my work. At least, I have not tried to force the issue. Whenever I have pushed any such concept in too obvious a manner, the resulting work has invariably been mediocre, if not, in retrospect, downright embarassing. I prefer to remain a little bit vague, a touch surreal. It suits me better.

When I was invited to submit work for a show relating in theme to the Pandora myth, I immediately realised that virtually the whole body of my work might well be appropriate. However, during the past year or so I have tried to steer some ideas towards the theme. The resulting work interprets, albeit loosely, the notion of Pandora's releasing, upon opening the Box, all manner of evils and misfortune. I have tried to depict a small sample of these.

Severed Head
Watercolour, 11 x 11 ins.

Jane Lewis

Joanne Woodward

The myth of Pandora is similar to the story of the fall of man, in that it is an attempt to explain the imperfections that exist in the world, why we do not live in an ordered paradise that we imagine to have existed.

I am not necessarily concerned with the role that woman is seen to play in these myths. I do not take personal offence as a woman, as I see the mythological woman to be only playing a symbolic part. She at worst represents a very powerful figure in these myths. It is after all Pandora who brings the box to earth and Eve who tempts Adam to eat the apple.

Whether Pandora's Box contains the wisdom of God or is full of evil, it is interesting that woman in these stories is given God-like powers stretching into the destiny of the world, considering that when these stories were invented man dominated over woman. Pandora is surely a contradiction to the stereotype of woman as the gentler sex? And isn't this yet another example of how the simplification of human nature into male and female traits is ignorant?

I see modern man as as much of a victim of stereotyping as woman, and if woman really is seen as the gentler sex dominated by man, then man must be continually struggling for power.

In the story of Adam and Eve, 'Adam's curse is to toil in the sweat of his brow', namely the labour the male associates with civilisation. Eden was a fantasy world without either effort or activity, which the entrance of the female with her sexuality destroyed.

Eve's sentence is far more political in nature and a brilliant 'explanation' of her considered inferior status. 'In sorrow thou shalt bring forth children. And thy desire shall be to thy husband. And he shall rule over thee'.

It is impossible to assess exactly how deeply embedded in our consciousness, these stories are; however the following lines from a Greek tragedy may show the effects in their most far reaching extreme :

The Two sins and five Slices
Mixed media

'The mother is not the parent of the child
Which is called hers. She is the nurse
Who tends the growth
Of young seed planted by its true parent
The male.
So if fate spares the child, she keeps it as one might
Keep for some friend a growing plant . . . .
Father without mother may beget . .
Aeschylus.

Today our earlier views towards birth must surely be very different, has not Eve rid herself of the curse placed on her in Eden: 'In sorrow thou shalt bring forth children'. For today she has the choice whether to bring forth a child or not.

The Milk Maid's Refusal is a dark look into medieval concsiousness. The original idea was a poem I wrote using lines out of some romantic poetry I found. When I put the lines in a certain order they seemed to evoke the wonder of coming life in the womb through momentary lust and its disposal into nothingness through abortion :

Who gave the O beauty
The keys to these breasts
Too credulous lover
Of blest unblest
Say, when in lapsed ages
The knew I of old
Or, what was the service
For which I was sold.

I drank of they fountain
False waters of thirst
Thou intimate stranger
The last and first.

Moan of Creation
Rapture that stirs
Blindly they learnt it
Years upon years.

And through the uncreated
Uncleft, untrod,
Breathed for a moment
The sorrow of God.

And lo! it fell starlike
Trembling to cease
In his infinite gladness
Infinite peace.

I find it difficult to see woman to have totally fallen victim to myths deeply embedded in our cultural inheritence, having lost any inhibitions that I might have had, as far as being a woman is concerned.

I enjoyed portraying Eve as the shrewd seductress, for if man idealises any woman as a sex symbol he falls victim to his own invention.

In *The Garden of Separate Circumstance*, the Pandora myth is combined with The Garden of Eden. Eve/Pandora clad in a saucy minidress emerges out of a vessel which could be seen as Pandora's Box. Adam stands cumbersone weighed down with his crown in awe of the sexy untouchable Eve.

The Two sins and five Slices takes the theme further; Adam waits dreamily at the trunk of the forbidden tree, where Eve sits plump and satisfied in the branches. She is indifferent to her suitors who frantically bring her flowers, and she ignores Adam's serenade.

Cupid hovers above, and we may see the possible outcome of the situation in the perfect equal union of man and woman. This is seen at the top of the picture in the symbol of King and Queen with child. This is an alchemical symbol representing the two having become a single being, and the child born to the royal pair symbolizes the philospher's stone, which in alchemy is an idea of perfection or perfect harmony.

The Erasmian Pyxis

In *The Erasmian Pyxis* I tried to tell the story of Pandora's Box in pictures and lead them up to present day. The painting is purposely dark and obscured as if it is something vague and dug up but not quite understood.

The far left panel shows the beginnings of mankind and Prometheus is stealing fire from Heaven. There are glimpses of what is to become the outcome of Prometheus's action in the deposition of Christ from the cross shown at the bottom of the picture.

The far right panel shows Pandora

The Erasmian Pyxis
Mixed media

coming to earth in a parachute. This is a happy occasion for it is on this day that fantasy is born, and the women who are birthing are released from their constant labour.

The centre left hand panel shows the opening of Pandora's Box releasing tremendous energy and the question mark which is to hover over mankind for ever, the question of his existence, (where did he come from and why?).

The right of centre panel shows the consequence of the opening of the box; modern life as we know it today. However behind all this lies hope.

Joanne Woodward

Hilary Rosen

Hilary Rosen

I was brought up in the centre of London near Kilburn, and lived in a block of pe-war mansion flats. I had quite a lively childhood. Often taken to Lyons Corner House for tea on Sundays, or taken round the big stores in Oxford Street, I was often surrounded by crowds of people bustling about. I was quite aware of different types of people from an early age. I remember a newspaper seller outside Oxford Street station, who had a distorted, scarred face, and being quite fascinated by this, and just stared at him. That image now reminds me of a Grosz drawing; also I recall the red-lipsticked ladies smelling of face powder and dressed in black who sold millinery in the shops. So a lot of these images of people in cafes, streets and shops are imprinted on my mind.

One set of grandparents lived in Cable Street, E.1. I remember the area as being badly bombed. Crumbling, devastated homes littered the streets. There were no trees. Just the sombre darkness of a dilapidated area, surrounded by corrugated iron fencing. In my grandparents' flat – they lived above a butcher's shop which was small and cosy – I remember it being mainly of beige and brown colours. An old oak table with turned legs covered in a brown, tasselled chenille tablecloth stood in the centre of the room and was covered with fruit and sweets. There were cats and dogs who nestled together in front of the fire and chicken soup being cooked on a stove in the kitchen. Both my grandparents were quiet, warm, kind, religious people, quite poor and almost humble.

In contrast to this environment my other grandparents lived quite an opulent life. My Nan had been a dancer on the stage, coming from a large, poor, Irish family. She was put on the stage at an early age and sang and danced in the cinema and on ships' cruises. So she and all her brothers and sisters were dancing and performing in troupes, or were theatrical agents.

Heavy brocade curtains hung from the windows and the furniture was covered in rich embossed green and

Tug of war
Charcoal on paper, 34 x 27 ins.

red velvet with a flowered pattern. She had wardrobes full of brightly coloured and textured clothes which she never wore any more. She would never dream of going out unless she wore a matching velvet hat with hat pins. Paste and real jewellery would be glistening and tinkling around her. Often there would be large gatherings of her family, henna'ed haired aunts and uncles talking in loud stage whispers during tea and fingering the tablecloths.

This environment on the one hand has given me a passion for colour, pattern and paste jewellery. But also when I was older, an assessment of different life styles and social inequalities became prevalent.

Later on at art college, I would spend a great deal of time drawing quick sketches of people in cafes, streets and parks. This developed a quick line and a general physiognomy. I find that you can only draw from what you know and you can only 'know' by drawing it. This quick drawing of imagery is an invaluable source of ideas.

Another influence on my work has been working with people. At present I teach for I.L.E.A. in a day centre and hospital. Before that while at college, I worked as a care assistant in an elderly people's home and also a hospital. This gave me the opportunity of again meeting a different type of person and experiencing a different reality.

These elements I have described have been the general influences on me; one can go on describing the effects of war, poverty in the Third World disease and aggression – all these elements are part of our existence which inevitably effect us.

I shall now go on to talk about the historical influences on my work. **Again there is a whole gamut of paintings, ideas, sculptures which**

I relate to, but I feel Grosz, Kollwitz and Shahn have been the most immediate inspirations.

Grosz has a marvellous line and use of watercolour depicting his characters. His views on prostitutes are, I feel, quite mysogonistic – he saw them as pampering to men's sexual needs but I feel they are more victims of society. But again, Grosz was cynical about the Weimar Republic anyway.

I am a great admirer of Kathe Kollwitz for the reason that she was a woman artist having children and organising her life around this. Also because of her subject matter and media – stark black and white. While she was in Munich, she was taught by Max Klinger. He stated: 'some themes should be drawn rather than painted, they would be ineffective or even inartistic if rendered by means of painting. The graphic arts could better express the darker aspects of life'. Looking at Kathe Kollwitz's work, the imagery she used seems more relevant in 1980's society than it did even ten years' ago, especially her drawings of poverty and unemployment which she drew for the magazine *Simplicissimus*.

Her subjects of women and children have, in my opinion, more insight than many other interpretations of the subject. She doesn't romanticise the role of motherhood, but shows the image of mother as a protector, survivor, a strength, and emotional and physical provider. She is the one who has to continue, no matter what tragedy befalls her.

The other artist I would like to mention is Ben Shahn, an American who was dedicated to humanitarianism, and social issues. Shahn was more of a painter, mainly using tempera and oils. He depicts the social conditions of the poorer areas of the USA and its inhabitants in the 1930s and 1940s.

There is a wide range of art history that has been influential in my work. But my own preferences, from my experiences and observations are painting, sculpture, photography and ideas that have a social/humanitarian subject matter, coupled with colour, pattern and texture.

Untitled

Now to finally discuss the imagery in 'Pandora's Box', which is probably self-explanatory.

I took the image of Pandora as being a contemporary woman. Although she opened the box and let out evils (so the myth goes), she is also the symbol of hope, and as I see it most of the evils are created by males.

We see Pandora as hope, and according to the Greek myth, 'hope had golden wings', so here she is amongst the multi-racial, men women and children of society who represent hope, peace and the future. The antithesis of this are the evils flying out of the box. Aggressive soldiers, torture, alcoholism and poverty, beaten men and women and nuclear rockets, filling the atmosphere with death and destruction.

Hilary Rosen

Define 'MYTH' . . . 'A legend, magnified by tradition, and given out as historical, affecting the origin of a race or a religion, and expressive of primitive beliefs or forms of belief: a fable, an invention'.
Nuttals Standard Dictionary.
'MYTH' . . . 'The Noble Lie' . . . Plato.

A myth is a fiction . . . yet, myths shape our knowledge, and comprehension of the world.

My interest in, and what I consider to be the significance of 'Pandora's Box' is the psychological import of this. myth – in creating an image of the Female, which today still surrounds, and demeands, any female person.

First: how did the Greeks travel in concept, from Gaia, the omnipotent, female, sole creator of the universe – believed to have borne the first race of gods, and also gave birth to the human race – Pandora, the carrier of destruction – a negative concept. It is as if the story were an attempt to enhace male pride, and act as scape-goat for male conscience – a vain and negative thought. Yet to our misfortune, it has been quoted down through the centuries.

In fact, it is true to say, that all written history is guilty of playing down, or even negating, womans' responsible actions – as though to remove action itself, and critical insight, from her sphere.

REVIEWING MY WORK:

I detect an underlying anxiety, but also a faith in the enormous inner strengths a woman can command:

a recognition of the stringent boundaries – such as that very fact: denigration of status through image-giving, male-created myths, plus, an assertion of self-contained endurance, and power. I can only approach the 'theme' by recreating my Pandora, in my terms, to be this self-motivated, freedom-seeking, human being – who shares the problems – joys and pains, of this world, with the rest of its, the worlds, creatures.

Regarding this exhibition, I ask myself: is there a difference of approach distinguishable between women and men when making art?

Drown the sound, 1983
Oil on canvas, 36 x 24 ins.

Or in my own attitude to art?

All artists work primarily from a special individual need, to make a plastic representation of the world about them. Visual art is a language in which to channel ones' thoughts and feelings: ones' vision, through the necessary balance of formal structure and self-expression.

Creativity, in the human soul, does not recognize sexual barriers. An artist is an artist – needing to speak. I hesitate to put barriers up, and make false divisions for art – as society has done for people.

But, the conventions of female and male lives have lain far apart – even in childhood, and through early education, girls are familiarised with the details of living, the intimacies, whereas boys are rarely encouraged to be even self-reflective, and are imbued with a certain pride – so that heroics have a resonance to them, which often ring hollow and false to the female mind particularly in this disillusioned age.

This is not to say that women are not idealistic, and will fight for these ideals – since an intelligent mind will always seek out a moral code for living.

But I think that the parallel lines I am talking about, in our background life – patterns can be seen to exist in certain areas of the practice of art today. For instance, I doubt there would be a female Schnabel – it would not be worth her while, to produce hombastic objects, empty of all but peacock display.

As a generality, and according to the current rules of the game, many male artists would be satisfied to make a 'career' in art – where many female artists, whose chances of making a 'career' are so negligible, must work from a different premise – an urgent inner need to comment on the world, or explore their own consciousness.

I have always worked from some inner need, aiming to comprehend reality better myself, knowing that others might gain insight also, by rearranging the signs, and evolving images.

As an artist, I attempt to give woman a fresh image in art – but will it be 'acceptable' to society (male) – or will It be edited out, 'peripheral', as other women artists through history. Will future art history record, and respect, the images made by women artists – of themselves, of men, of ideas?

Clearing the ropes, 1984
Oil on canvas, 60 x 48 ins.

Maria Chevska

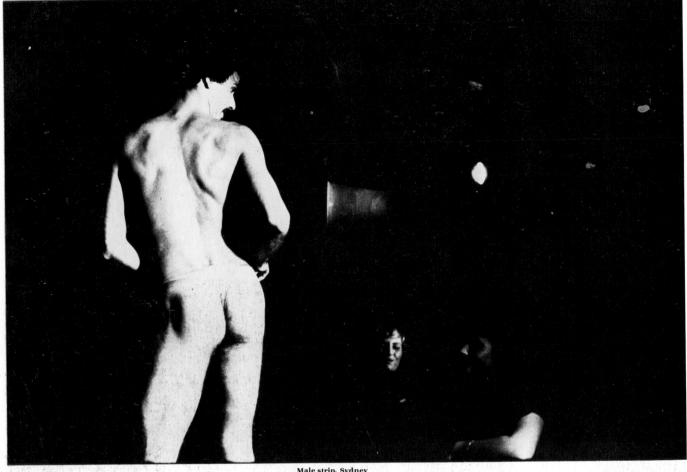

Male strip, Sydney
Photograph

Some people still think that the women's movement is about women wanting to *be* men, rather than wanting to be equal contributors to accepted meanings within society. These people seem to think that equality will come either when women behave exactly as men do, or when their behaviour will be a kind of mirror-image of men's, a female version of men's.

This peculiar attitude manifests itself in the kind of role-reversal which is expected to take place in the male strip club.

The Pandora legend is about guilt . . . that women, Pandora, Eve, are made responsible for contaminating the world . . . and we women must forever try to expiate that guilt. But of course when we examine most of the things plaguing us today we realize that they originate with men . . .

So it's nice to consider that the legend was wrong. Perhaps another projection or role-reversal that doesn't work.

The lights go down. A spotlight catches the first glimpse of a gyrating young man, dark and muscular, moving between the women's tables to the beat of disco music. Suddenly, he motions to a seated well-dressed women in her mid-twenties to join him on stage. She refuses at first, but then, encouraged by her girl friends, she moves on to the stage, hesitantly, and in a kind of improvised dance, unbuttons his shirt and drops it onto the floor to the applause of her friends. She returns to her table grinning with a mixture of relief and satisfaction. She has just had her initiation into the male strip.

An evening of this kind is becoming increasingly popular. It attracts women of all ages and backgrounds. What draws women to this event? Is it revenge, or just curiosity? Is the evening a playful re-enactment of women's fantasies or suppressed desires? Is it possible to reverse sexual roles, even just for one night? Do men and women's views of an event of this kind differ?

The director of the evening, an American in his late twenties, chose

the five male strippers 'not only for
their looks but their personalities.' The
dancers act as waiters prior to their
stage appearances. They have a scrubbed, wholesome appearance.

By the time the men perform, the
women, well-fed and filled with
alcoholic camaraderie, are encouraged
to laugh at themselves and at the men
as they perform a kind of comic mock
strip. Any element of eroticism is
subdued as the women laugh at the
temerity and bravado of the other
women, and the 'come hither' antics
of the men.

Modelled on male strip evenings in
the United States, is there anything
particularly Australian about the
evening? One dancer that had worked
both in the United States and Australia
said that he felt 'Australian women
were much rowdier.' One performer,
an aerobics instructor, said that he had
appeared in shows where the women
'chased the men around the room.'

Another women said, 'there were
very few places that they could go for
an all-women's night without being
hassled by men . . . so that was one
reason they chose to come to the
strip . . . and it wasn't a very interesting
evening. Sydney beaches were more
interesting.'

Male strip, Sydney
Photograph

Joyce Agee

Male.strip, Sydney
Photograph

Does an evening of this kind serve as a barometer of the current state of society or of sexual roles? Colin Whelan, Sydney photographer, took photographs of the male strip for a gay publication in the city. He felt that it was an 'index of the change in the way Australian men view themselves – less embarrassed and freer in themselves to express themselves.' He did admit to being surprised at the youth of the women attending the evening and also how outrageously some of the women behaved.

It is probably a shared view that the male strip reflects superficial changes in men and women's roles, generally and in Australia. However, I think it shows another way in which the emancipation of women is neutralized, thus becoming just another commercial proposition.

Joyce Agee

In sorting through personal recollections of my own experiences or the experiences of close friends, the single most obvious area of life affected is that of responsibility for sexual attraction and its consequences. This starts relatively young in the training that a girl should be 'pleasing to look at', totally innocent or 'unconscious of their own sexuality (never mind anybody elses) and in general 'above suspicion', i.e., never seen to be instigators of sexual activity. Pandora was, after all, and this has been doted on by everyone, innocent of intentional wrong-doing, curiosity not being, of itself, a crime. Otherwise she would be a 'witch'. Two examples, from early puberty:

Age 12:   Dressing up to go out to dinner. Sitting at table with parents, bored. Interest lands on the figure of a man at nearby table. Staring until interrupted by mother who has noticed and is, by then, furious. Daughter is taken home abruptly and locked up with angry accusations such as 'slut', 'whore', 'the way you were looking at that man', etc.

Age 12-14 (somewhere in there): Fascinated by a handiman who was working round the place, she hung around him. His response-sexual arousal and physical advances towards her. He hurt her . . . and scared her. She ran to her father, reporting this crime and seeking consolation. Her father asked her to confess what she had done to the handiman.

and on and on and one. Innocence must be maintained and guilt is assumed. The battle goes on and on. A little later, when the female population acquires access to money, they are encouraged to contribute a large portion of it to the 'beauty industry'. To create a consumer need where there was none two years previously, the industry encourages girls to feel

Pandora
Suite of five photo-etchings
8 x 8 ins.

inadequate, also inviting confessions to this effect, and then offers to 'help'. It is, by that age assumed that an important function for the female will be to 'lure men' and that this is best done through physical appearance.

I do relate this, and have been very brief about it, to the adverse effects of stories like Pandora's Box, where a female figure is either a pawn in the struggle between male powers, or an idiot-child who is not to be trusted with larger matters. I have also presented her in an alternative role.

Deborah Monroe

Pandora, the gift to all – the all-gifted – represents, aside from the obvious 'beautiful object', the fascination/attraction, fear/repulsion conflict inherent in the sexual 'other'. Made in heaven – a treacherous gift. As the first of a race of women she carried with her, from the start, the power to attract and the invisible womb – part of herself hidden . . . a very significant part . . . a secret box. A man could lose himself there . . . would eventually find his way there . . . but might not return . . . or return changed. He might lose something there. The general name for what might be lost is CONTROL and once lost there might be HAVOC, which is almost always considered synonymous with evil and catastrophe.

It's no small wonder that this combination of self-sufficient beauty (for she was both master of the arts and an object of great beauty) and perilous danger should be an act of vengeance from above, from Zeus to Epimetheus for his brother's transgression. Whereas fire enabled the establishment of communities and social order, the gradual domination of man over nature the counterpart – or 'fly in the soup' – was the introduction of Pandora. Men could lose their minds (rationality) over her – be carried off by their senses – both emotionally – since she is also the child-bearing mother – and sexually – since attraction to her means seeking out the Box.

I tend to see her as one of the strongest symbols of male fantasy. Neither castration complex nor the somewhat flat and unimaginative notion of woman as sex object, but rather Pandora as the personification of intangible sexual and sensual arousal – a figment of the imagination insofar as communication with her – a

and the golden hair. (I don't consider her a teen-age or child tease, as she is often presented by men). It's an open and receptive position, rather more self-contemplating than seeking. Child-bearing is not her only power, but may, in fact, be the only one for which she is not condemned – the 'hope' that remained for man after the box was opened may well be seen as the possibility he recognised for saving himself through reproduction in her womb.

The box, invisible in the first instance, represents the varying degrees in the superstructure of rationality and logic inherent in rational and social organisation and which *can* all but block out the memory of the offering.

Deborah Monroe

give and take relationship – is not possible. One can give nothing to the all-gifted, nor be as one with the sexual 'other', and the uncontrollable desire to do so – which SHE inspires, leads to havoc, and eventually through despair to two possibilities for the male – self-destruction or destruction of her. She is sensuality, the arts and the imagination – the allusive butterfly, so to speak – a part of the self very much unaware of the constructs of material possession and the consequences of tampering with them.

I have presented her here in five relationships to the box. These may not only be the varying relationships to sensual offering and the fear of loss that tries to blot it out or impose a material or rational superstructure on it that I think men feel toward woman, but in many respects which each individual may feel towad their own sexuality. I have presented her in a fertility position with open hands, palms outward – THE OFFERING – anonymous save for the female body

Marisa Rueda

When we decided to work on the theme 'Pandora's Box' I never thought that it was going to be so ideologically intricate (it always happens when one approach events with old preconceptions). When my work was chosen for 'Women's Images of Men' I thought that it was a good opportunity to exhibit, though I never before gave any relevance to group exhibitions ('one person exhibitions are the ones that count') nor did I ever receive any feed-back from them.

Not only did I change this idea after the exhibition, I also became more

feminism and political awareness were essential to re-shaping attitudes, that as artists we must be in the front line to bring back the sense of the value of each life. My tortured victim was strung in the window, and each day as the Malvinas/Falklands crisis deepened I added the day's newspaper's '500 HEROS', 'SHEFFIELD SUNK', etc. From the buses and cars people could see this dead body and the headlines. Even through the grille at night, people got the message. At the same exhibition Deborah Law was speaking of Greenham Common in a

myth. For me Pandora's Box brought childhood images of fairy tales, the myth was confused with 'Ali Baba', the exotic east, this beautiful and inquisitive woman who opened the jar letting vapours of different colours flow out. As a child I did not have any concept of the world's evils, only these vapours and the irreversability of disobedience.

How our important women's roles have been mystified by fear and repression! This myth is an image of women which has been provoked by fear and the necessity to

Akewa's Road to Freedom
Ceramic figures

aware of women's position in society and maybe more important I met other women, and the solitary process of creation and building was shared. Elena Samperi and I began a project in which several women artists, using different artistic media, could work on the same theme, elaborating similar and different ideas, sometimes borrowing images from each other's work and retranslating into one's own piece. At the moment the two of us share a studio and we are still nurturing this idea.

When in April 1982, Argentina and England went to war, I fled to Holland to think, but returned to join my feminist friends in a political show called 'At the Crossroads'. We saw in reactions to that show, from both casual passers-by and those who had come to see an art exhibition, that

collage with women's letters worrying about a nuclear holocaust. 'At the Crossroads' was an idea of Joyce Aggee. 'Power Plays' came afterwards with Jacqueline Morreau, Sue Coe and me. The exhibition was put together by Bryan Biggs (director of the Blue Coat Gallery, Liverpool). He says: 'Their individual approaches to making are quite distinct, however they are linked thematically here by a shared concern for aspects of power – political, regligious, patriarchal – and the ways in which it is abused'.[1]

So . . . a lot came from 'Women's Images of Men'.

Returning to the myth. It took me a long time to reach the concept of this new work: firstly because of my political background that produced a different imagery and second because I found it difficult to modify an old

oppress – from being considered objects and being presented like gifts – to being considered unworthy, untruthful, inquisitive; objects of desire, guilty of the feelings that are provoked in the oppressor/desirer.

All the modifications I thought for near a year were in words. I was beginning to work and only concepts were appearing. Where are the images going to come from?

I was very fortunate to meet Diane Dossorr in Liverpool last spring. She organized a women's visual arts conference at the college where she teaches. We became friends and she sent me this photocopy from a book she was reading *Ancient Mirrors of Womanhood* by Merlyn Stone and the goddess in this myth is called Akewa.

This unique account of women's arrival upon earth, from the Toba people of Argentina, is one that may linger in the minds of many women, as we struggle to comprehend the senseless violence of both rape and war. Though images of the Goddess in many cultures of Central and South America is as the moon, the Toba reverse the situation, regarding the sun as the Goddess, the moon as male. The ability of Akewa to grow young, as well as old, may be compared to the Navajo concepts of 'Changing Woman'.

Who has not heard of that most ancient time when women descended from the heavens, climbing down the great rope that hung from the sky to walk upon the earth, searching for new plants and roots that they might carry back to their home in the heavens?
And who has not heard that when the women arrived the men were still animals, their bodies covered with fur, walking upon their hands as well as their feet? So it was that chancing upon the rope whose end touched the brown soil, the animals jumped at it and snapped it with their teeth – so that the women from heaven were forced to remain upon the earth. It was in this way that the women of heaven and the male animals of earth began to live side by side and upon their mating with each other, they brought forth the people who now live upon the Toba lands. Yet one woman still lives in the heavens for each day we see the fiery Akewa as She climbs from the lowest part of heaven to walk across the wide skies, bringing us Her golden light and warmth, giving us the gift of Her brilliant being – until She travels so far to the other side that She slides into the abyss at the end of the world, leaving us for the night.[2]

At the time I was thinking of following up my new figures of the oppressors, shown last year in 'Power Plays', with a *Merry go round of generals*, and began to build the figures for it. Clergymen, informers, policemen, they began to run, to escape, to bite each other. The military coup of Argentina began to lose economical and political grounds and finished losing even professional respect from the people with their defeat in the Malvinas war.

They had to call for elections in my country and a democratic government is in action now though not necessarily in power.

So . . . I felt that Akewa, in my work, gets free from all the power men bring and releases herself from a military suit and stiletto shoe as she goes up joyfully reach freedom. She faces the Universe, her own birth, free from roles, clothes, duties, happy to be a life. She is me, she is my daughter, she is my mother.

But be careful, they are still there as a constant menace, this people in power, a true menace, not only to women but to men of good will who really want changes and freedom.
Can't you see them walking over El Salvador, Grenada, Nicaragua, Latin America . . . Everywhere?

1. Foreward by Bryan Biggs from the catalogue of *Power Plays* 1983.
2. *Ancient Mirrors of Womanhood* by Merlyn Stone.

Marisa Rueda

Mary McGowan

Mary McGowan

'Myth' is a tender word; it breathes off the lips with such gentle reassurance that the strength and brutality it carries can hardly be comprehended. Our lives are constructed on so many myths and images that are destructive to our self-image. In the same way that we are breaking down social myths and stereotypes so also we must examine and reintepret the basic myths even though they seem remote and irrelevant to twentieth century life. Ancient myths of creation and social ordering still carry weight in our heritage.

Untitled
Oil on canvas, 30 x 40 ins.

A myth is a weapon, it is a way of explaining and ordering the universe. Better to use that weapon by examining and reinterpreting myths that are unsympathetic to women.

Myths are alive in that they can become more or less powerful and relevant but also because they can be developed. Pandora's Box is a curiously ambiguous myth. Historically it has been regarded as a satire on women. Pandora, the first woman is created by the craftsman Hephaestus on the orders of Zeus to punish man for having received the gift of fire from the rebellious god Prometheus. An

apparently passive figure in a drama directed by three male gods, she is blessed or cursed with curiosity to open the box. From this all the troubles of the world fly out and before she can close the lid all that remains in the box is hope.

As a satire Pandora's Box is somewhat implausible. It does not suggest any idea of Paradise before the Fall, such as the Eve and Adam myth. Curiosity is hardly an evil, on the contrary, it is a very positive attribute. So, we can begin to rework the myth into a more plausible pattern.

Prometheus is no longer the independent hero, the existential rebel, defier of gods and benefactor of mankind. He has now become a one-dimensional, cocksure, arrogant petty thief. He is consumed with the single idea of his own importance and his one solitary gift of fire.

Pandora is no longer an instrument of divine punishment. Her wilfulness is assertive. Her enquiring mind releases evil and good to full examination. She gives mankind the full range of qualities, doubt and pain, joy and understanding. She is the real existential hero because she gives mankind the ability to choose.

I grew up in Muff, a village in County Donegal, which is artificially cut off from its main city Derry by the partition of Ireland. Village life in Ireland is common to all, even city dwellers regard themselves as part of tight small communities. Muff was the first stopping off point for the youth of Derry on a Friday night and with the beginning of the Troubles, it became more popular as an escape from the oppressive military presence in the North. At this time I identified very much with the Civil Rights movement especially because it was led by a woman – Bernadette Devlin.

Two things which were obvious while I was growing up were the discrimination against Catholics living in Northern Ireland in terms of opportunities, education and jobs, and the general discrimina-

tion against women in all Irish society. The repressive trinity of Church, State and family have combined to ensure that progress for women in that island is painful and slow.

The few institutions in Northern Ireland strong enough to resist religious bigotry and discrimination towards women are the Colleges and Universities. By the time I went to Belfast in 1972 the Civil Rights Movement had declined, the army was well entrenched and the mood in the colleges had become more inward

Bar Scene
Oil on canvas, 30 x 36 ins.

looking. So in the confines of the college it was possible to ignore the growing bitterness of politics.

Feminism never seemed to penetrate the consciousness with the force that it could have. It was then generally dismissed as a middle class phenomenon from across the water. Within the Art and Design Centre itself two women were appointed to the existing eight male members of staff in the Fine Art Department. This was regarded as a big step forward at the time. Life in Belfast deteriorated as sectarian violence grew. Safe and 'No Go' areas were clearly defined and continual interruptions, bomb scares and body searches became part of routine daily life.

For the unemployed would-be artist Belfast was no city and London was the natural place to go. The relative freedom of a cosmopolitan city was and still is in many respects intoxicating.

Eve
Oil on canvas, 30 x 36 ins.

Mary McGowan

LEWIS BIGGS

Pandora and Pandemonium

Most people, I hope, in simply enjoying this exhibition will accept the reasons for its existence as self-evident. But for anyone who finds it surprising, and for those of us who have been concerned for two or three years over how to make it happen, I want to say why, for me, Pandora's Box is so unusual and important.

It is not hard to be horrified by the problems humanity has made for itself in the world, and, now, above it. Artists, like anyone else, are affected by that horror; and, in additin to provoking some of them to try to find political and other remedies for those problems when they are not working, many of them also express a sense of horror, or the hope of release from it, in their work. There have been times, particularly during the economic boom of the nineteen-sixties, when 'serious' issues were unfashionable in 'serious' art. While many artists then sought freedom from such issues, now more often they must fight for art to be taken seriously when it does concern itself int his way. Artists who have something important to express can find a useful ally in myths – stories which have proved their fundamental explanatory power over many generations, despite being retold in many different ways according to the particular conditions of the society in which they are told.

There are reasons enough in the story why Pandora should have been a particular inspiration to the artists contributing to this exhibition. If there are artists who are men who have been similarly inspired, perhaps it is only just that they should have been omitted from the exhibition in the same way that Epimetheus is usually left out of the story.

Pandora's Box has been conceived and motivated by a small group of artists, bound together by nothing but their enthusiasm for promoting art which expresses the ways in which women are concerned about the world. An exhibition like this takes a huge amount of time, energy, expertise and money to arrange, and these things are not normally available all at the same time to people who are not 'professional' exhibition organisers. All professions develop standards of judgement, ethically and in terms of formal quality, which are intrinsic to the profession (medical, educational, military etc.) but may seem incomprehensible to 'lay' people. Almost as valuable as the theme, (the meaning of the art), in the realisation of this exhibition, is the fact that it has been artists, not exhibition organisers, who have been responsible for shaping and developing it, with the 'professionals' playing a minor role. As well as the power of the art to please or provoke, the way the exhibition has been moulded by the organisers has played a significant part in making it a refreshing, unusual and important event.

Lewis Biggs
Bristol February 1984